AMBERLEY

AMBERLEY PUBLISHING LTD

The Hill, Merrywalks
Stroud
Gloucestershire GL5 4EP
Telephone: 01453 847813
Fax:
E-mail: n.giles@amberley-books.com
Visit: www.amberleybooks.com

Dear Editor,

Please find enclosed a copy of Amberley Publishing's latest book(s). All our authors are available for talks and interviews, so please let me know if you would like to set up such a meeting. I would also be grateful if you could contact me if you plan to review the book(s).

Kind regards,

Nicki Giles

(Publicist)

Registered in England and Wales no. 5358552   Registered office 73 Wimpole Street, London, W1G 8AZ

LONGTON

THROUGH TIME

Mervyn Edwards

AMBERLEY PUBLISHING

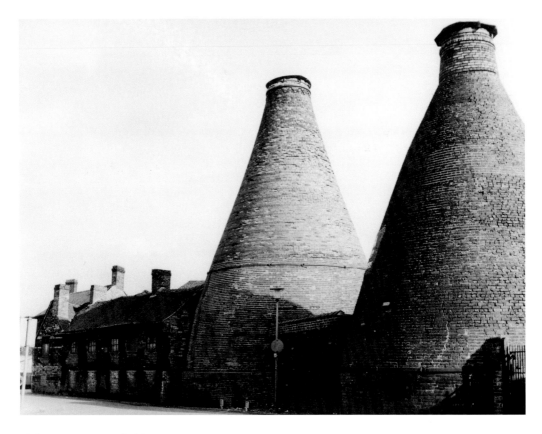

Elektra Pottery, Probably 1970s
The first known pottery works in Longton was the porcelain works at Longton Hall, built in the mid-eighteenth century. In the early nineteenth century, the town became the centre of the growing bone china industry. The Elektra Porcelain Company Ltd's works in Edensor Road was using the print mark Zanobia ware from 1924 and Vulcan ware from around 1940. The premises were demolished in 1975.

First published 2013

Amberley Publishing
The Hill, Stroud
Gloucestershire, GL5 4EP

www.amberley-books.com

Copyright © Mervyn Edwards, 2013

The right of Mervyn Edwards to be identified as the Author of this work has been asserted in accordance with the Copyrights, Designs and Patents Act 1988.

ISBN 978 1 4456 0816 7

British Library Cataloguing in Publication Data.
A catalogue record for this book is available from the British Library.

Typeset in 9.5pt on 12pt Celeste.
Typesetting by Amberley Publishing.
Printed in the UK.

Introduction

China Town is one of the more flattering titles that Longton has attracted over the years, and it's a name that recognises the town's peerless reputation for ceramic production. Big businesses such as Bridgwood, Aynsley, Webberley, Wild and Tams all flourished, the pottery firing process being aided by the so-called 'long-flame coals' particular to the Longton collieries. Surviving photographs of yawning marlholes speak volumes about the town's industrial past – a past that is splendidly interpreted at the Gladstone Pottery Museum in Uttoxeter Road.

The story of coal and clay in Longton is recalled in this book through numerous photographs of colliery buildings and fat-bellied bottle ovens. For people of a certain generation, it may be comforting to look back at these photographs, to be charmed by the cobbled courtyard of Gladstone and to rue the loss of pubs such as the Shamrock, the Waterloo and the Albion, However, to talk, *à la* A. E. Houseman, of the happy highways is to ignore certain truths about Longton.

It was prosperous but not pretty. The blue-sky thinking that led to the establishment of Queen's Park – a welcome lung for the town – was tempered by the unshakeable belief that the grey, smoky skies that prompted its arrival were a measure of Longton's affluence. John Aynsley, pottery manufacturer and town mayor, remarked with much pragmatism upon the opening of the park in 1888: 'They knew well that the noble town of Longton was smoky; but they generally considered in the town that where there was most smoke there was most cash.'

William Blake's early twentieth-century photographs of smoke-caked Longton speak volumes about its flourishing industry. The grimness of the town, its poor planning, the awkward, piecemeal development of factory sites and the rustic manners of downtrodden clay-workers pricked the curiosity of many a social commentator. Charles Knight acknowledged in 1847 that Longton had more potbanks than Burslem, and produced commoner wares. 'We have fancied, too, that the operatives have a somewhat stronger dash of roughness about them,' he adjoined.

Even as late as 1961, another outsider, Mervyn Jones, wrote that one local lad had told him that his mother wouldn't like it if he 'went with a Neck End girl'. Jones continued, 'Longton is supposed to be a rough place. It is also thought of as the most old-fashioned of the towns. It has the largest number of small, back-street potbanks, of potbanks which have failed, and of bottle ovens still in use.'

The old photographs in this book recall the heyday of the industrial town, but countless other images linger in the memory, recalling the Longton of yesteryear: redundant pottery workers drowning their sorrows in the bar of the Rose on Uttoxeter Road; the Workers' Educational Association (WEA) classes that ran in the Town Hall and the victorious fight to save the same building from demolition in 1985; and the tragedy of the Empire Theatre blaze on New Year's Eve, 1992.

Like so many of our local towns, Longton in 2013 is trying desperately to reinvent itself in the face of austerity cuts. It could do worse than take the advice of Clough Williams-Ellis, who built the Portmeirion village in Wales: 'Cherish the past, adorn the present and construct for the future.'

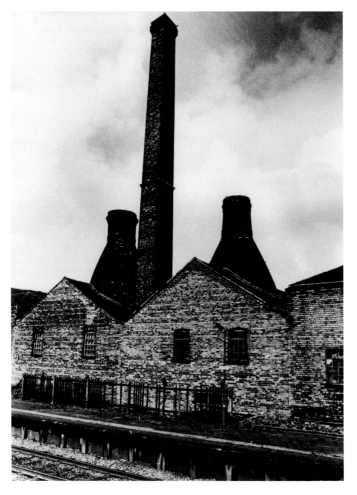

Phoenix Pottery Works, 1976
Here's a factory that stands as a not-untypical example of how a pottery factory's prosperity gave rise to additions and enlargement. Thomas Forrester began operating a modest factory business in High Street in 1877. It flourished, and so he took over additional buildings in Church Street. In time, these were replaced by a new factory on site, the Phoenix Works, completed in 1879. He subsequently bought the adjoining factory and combined the two works, thereby establishing a suitably large base for his thriving enterprise. Messrs Thomas Forester & Sons Ltd traded until 1959. The building still stands and is Grade II listed.

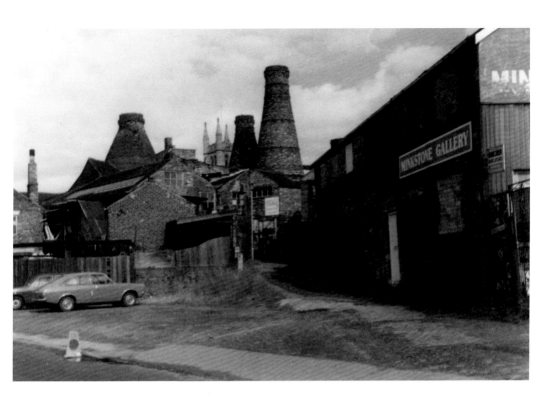

Short Street from Normacot Road, 1978 and 2013

Hanley has a Broad Street and Longton has a Short Street. It is situated between Uttoxeter Road and Normacot Road and is a winding street, paved with heavy blue dust bricks and standing in the shadow of the former Enson Works. Much conservation work has been carried out in recent years and mock Victorian gas lamps have been established in order to enhance its evocative setting. St James' church tower can be seen in the distance in the older photograph.

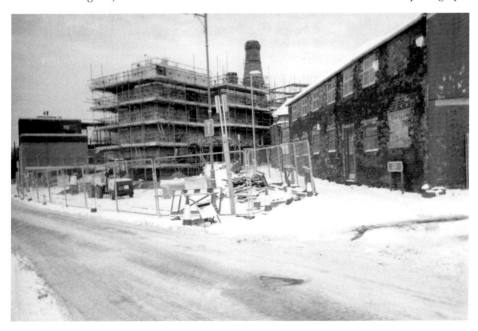

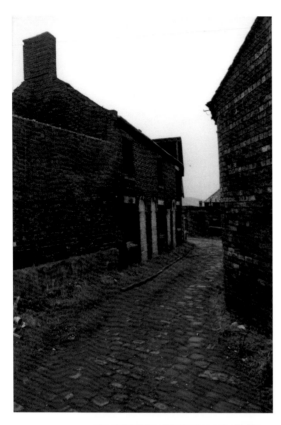

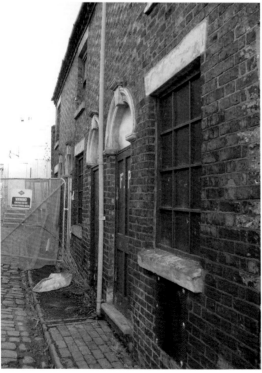

Short Street Cottages, *c.* 1980 and 2013
Three old cottages in Short Street
were Grade II listed in 1979, and are
believed to have once been workers'
dwellings. The cottages are viewed
from both the Uttoxeter Road end of
Short Street and from the Normacot
Road side. These dwellings were used
in the BBC adaptation of the 1910 novel
Clayhanger, by Arnold Bennett. Perhaps
no other area in the six towns illustrates
so faithfully the Potteries of the past.
Here, poky housing was juxtaposed
with an old factory and bottle ovens,
whose black smuts would have covered
the neighbouring houses. Short Street
and the immediate vicinity have been
designated a conservation area, though
the renovation of the adjacent Enson
Works for economically viable use has
been achieved with one eye on the
future as well as the past. The site is now
being used as a Centre of Refurbishment
Excellence (CORE).

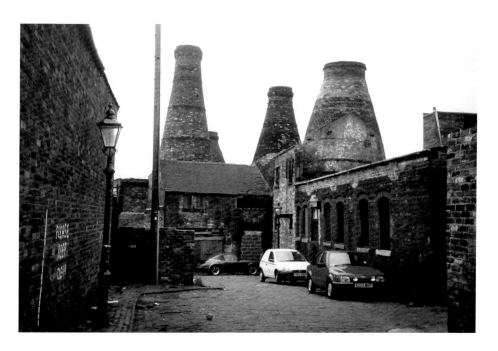

Short Street, 1997 and 2013

Another view of Short Street shows the nearby bottle ovens. It is estimated that there were 2,500 coal-fired kilns and ovens in operation before 1936, but with the adoption of cleaner fuels and the Clean Air Acts, ovens all over the Potteries were demolished. Only forty-seven remain in the city today, including those at Enson Works. Keith Meeson's Bottle Kiln Walk of 2009, organised as a fundraiser for the Donna Louise Trust, took in all the remaining ovens across the city.

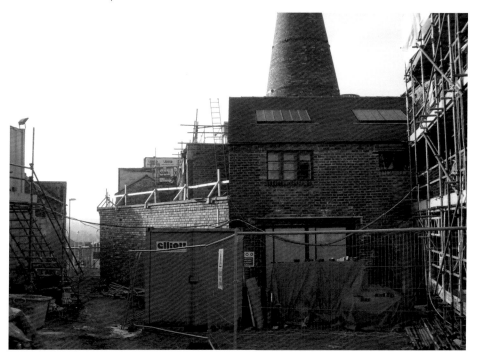

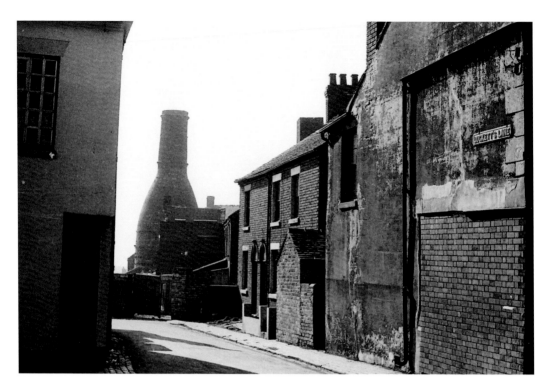

Lockett's Lane, Probably 1960s and 2013

Lockett's Lane was one of the slum areas of Longton by the late nineteenth century. The Victoria County History records that 'in the Edensor district, in John Street [now Calvin Street], in Lockett's Lane, and in the area around St James' church, conditions in the later nineteenth century were probably as bad as anywhere in the Potteries.'

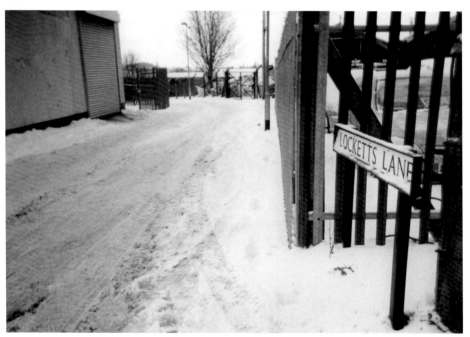

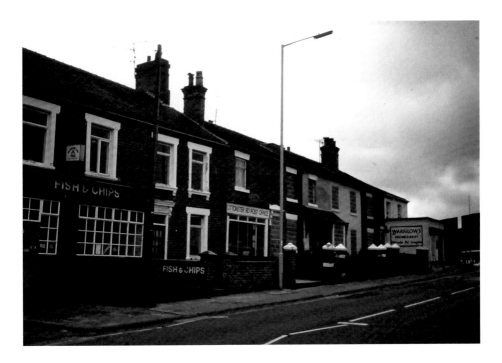

Uttoxeter Road, 1994 and 2013

Meer Lane is one of the old approach roads to Longton. The road is now Uttoxeter Road, and the town took on the name of Longton in the 1840s. In recent years, transport improvements and economic factors have triggered radical changes in Uttoxeter Road, such as the demolition of the properties above as well as the Station Hotel.

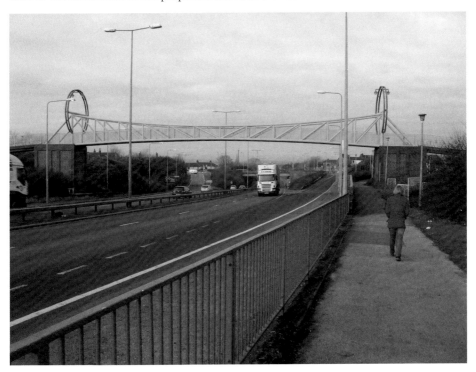

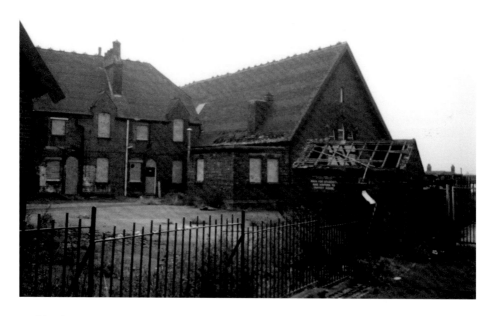

Webberley Lane, 1991 and 1997

Only six years separate these photographs, yet they illustrate what can be done with imagination and an injection of funding from the European Union. The former St James's School later became Tawney House, the branch office of the Workers' Educational Association. It was on the brink of being demolished when the city council extended a conservation area to include it and then transformed the building into the Hothouse Ceramic Design Centre. It was opened in early 1992.

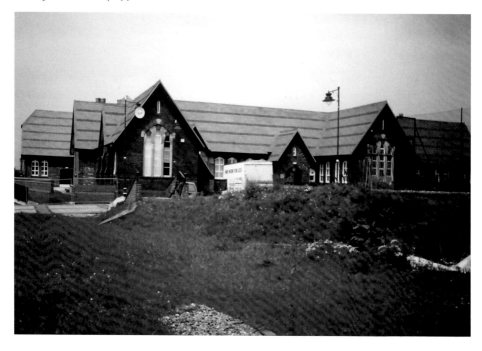

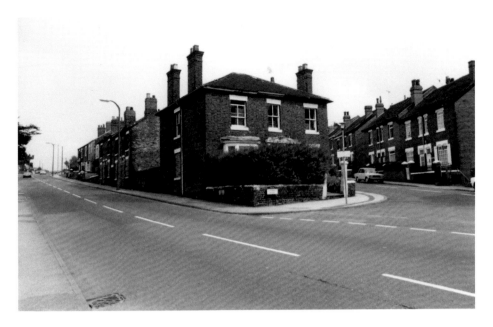

Upper Belgrave Road and Corner of Ludwall Road, *c.* 1980, and Same Site, 2013
Houses have been replaced with the Normacot Centenary Garden; its interpretative plaque
records: 'In the nineteenth century the Second Duke of Sutherland owned much of the land
in Normacot. He was instrumental in the building of the church and the school that stood
opposite and donating land for the Cottage Hospital. The Duke's Scottish connections are
reflected in road names – Rothesay, Argyle, Buccleigh and Hamilton, where homes were
built to his exacting model housing specifications.'

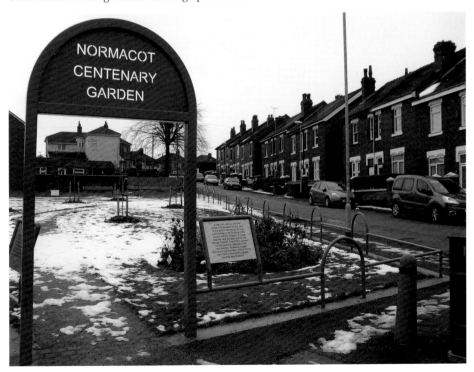

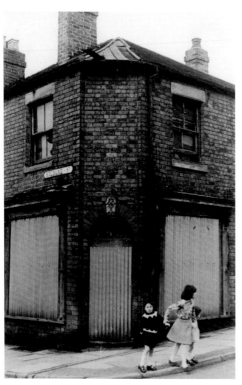

Kildare Street and Cromartie Street, Probably 1960s and 2013

When the Second Duke of Sutherland inherited Trentham Hall and estate in 1833, he was one of the most affluent men in the country, with an income of over £120,000 per annum. The commercial section of Porter's trade directory of 1887 lists the following people as among those living or trading in Kildare Street: Samuel Bentley, greengrocer; Alfred Brown, coal dealer; Thomas Degg, grocer, baker and outdoor beer-seller; Spencer Hampson, greengrocer; John Keay, coal and slack merchant; William Mills, grocer; Robert Parker, greengrocer; Charles Smith, cow keeper; and Eliza Spooner, draper. Within the fanlight over the doorway in the older photograph, we can just make out an advert for Typhoo tea.

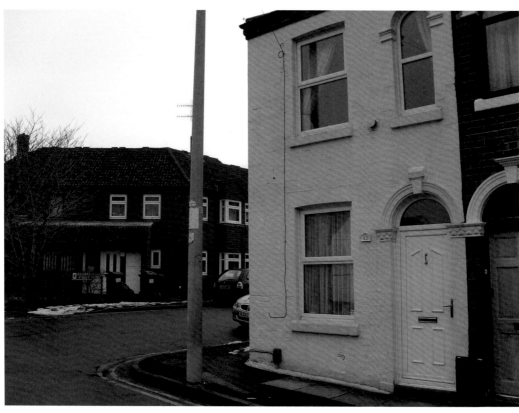

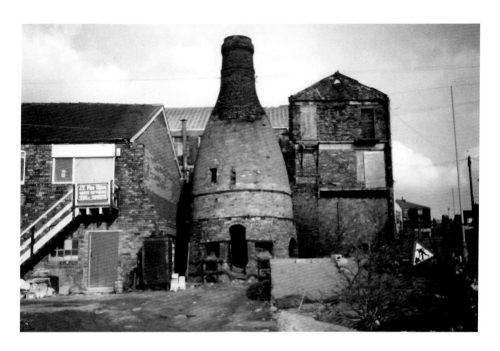

Normacot Road, 1994 and 2013

Early nineteenth-century Longton was known 'for the great irregularity in the position of its buildings of every size and sort, from the respectable residence of the manufacturer to the mud and saggar hovel of the pauper scattered over a wide extent of territory'. You never had to stroll too far around the streets to find a bottle oven. Here's one still standing in Normacot Road. J. T. Fine China traded on this site when the older photograph was taken.

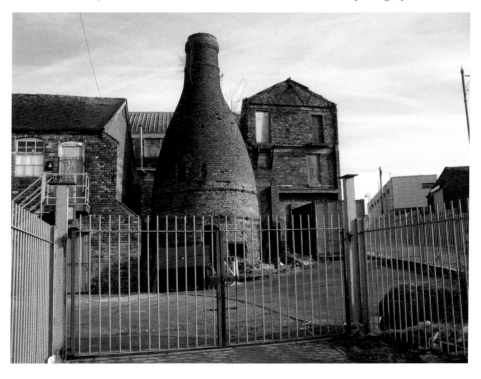

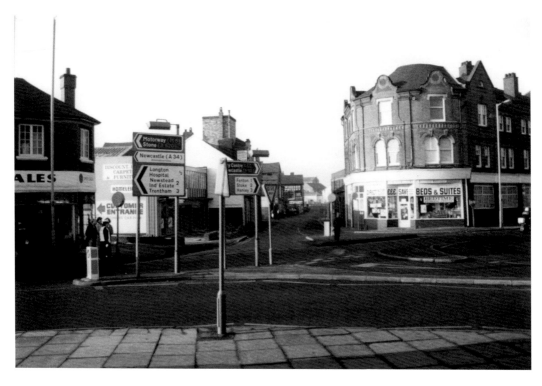

The Strand, Junction with Commerce Street, 1989 and 2013

Early twentieth-century photographs of Stafford Street, now known as the Strand, show its tramlines and Wesleyan chapel, now the site of the Central Hall. It was an important street, also embracing the Crown Works of John Tams Ltd and Bradley's pawnbroker's shop. Commerce Street was the address of the much-loved Empire Theatre, which was destroyed by fire on New Year's Eve 1992.

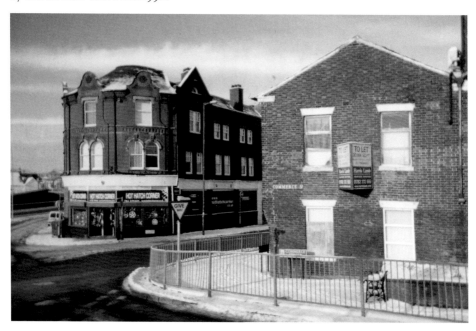

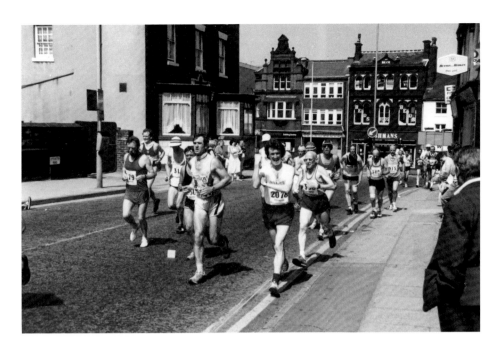

Uttoxeter Road, 1988 and 2012

The Potteries Marathon runners stream through the streets of Longton in the above photograph. The Union Hotel was a foremost venue in Longton prior to closure. Part of the road surface outside the hotel was made up of pieces of broken saggar up until the late 1870s. In 1864, George Slinn, a groom in the employ of Joseph H. Hawley, landlord, was caught drinking his employer's port in the hotel stables. He was sentenced to twenty-one days' imprisonment for theft.

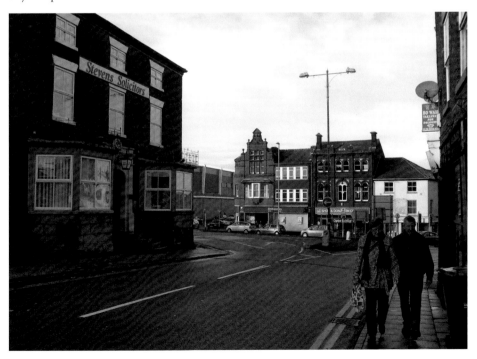

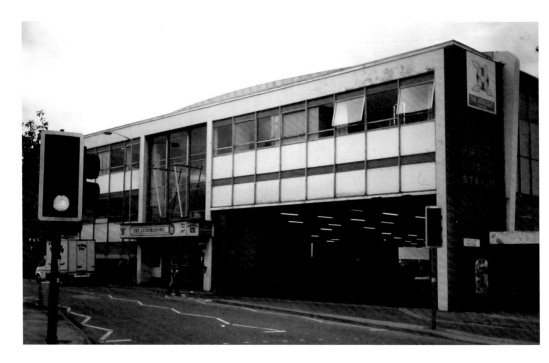

Bus Station, 1994 and 1997

Jollees was opened in 1973 in a former bowling alley above Longton bus station. Its location made it a very unlikely entertainment magnet, but over the years it attracted the top names in showbusiness: The Three Degrees, Des O'Connor, Les Dawson, Cliff Richard and more. It also played host to the World Darts Championships. It closed in 1981, ultimately becoming the leisurebowl, before reopening as the Jollees nightclub in 1997. The building was demolished in 2003.

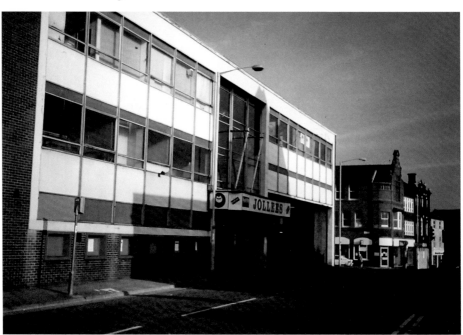

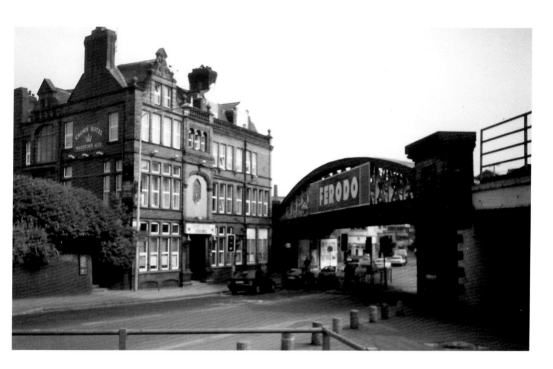

Crown Hotel, 1995 and 2013

The bottom view of the Crown Hotel is seen from the railway line, above. One day in July 1893, the Derby train arrived at 12.16 p.m. at Longton station with a man's head on the footplate of its engine. The body of Isaac Hall, who had been run over, was later discovered further down the line at Normacot. The resultant coroner's inquest concluded that Hall had been knocked down by the oncoming train while walking – rather foolishly – through the tunnel near Meir.

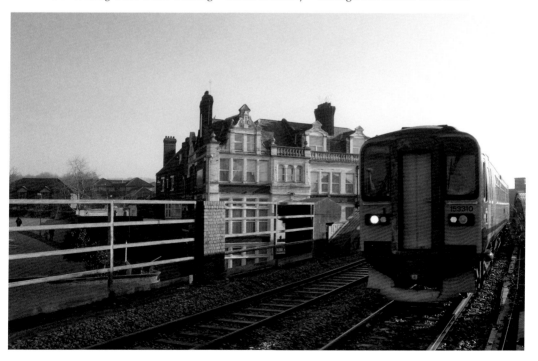

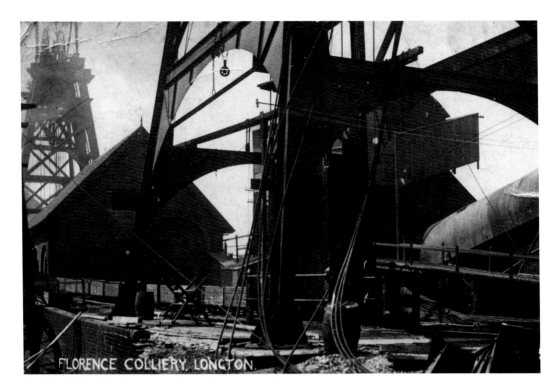

FLORENCE COLLIERY, LONGTON.

Florence Colliery, 1908 and 1994

Our section on coalmining begins with Florence Colliery, originally owned by the Duke of Sutherland and named after the 3rd Duke's eldest daughter. The colliery opened in 1874, the shafts having been sunk between 1872 and 1877. Our postcard shows the headsticks of No. 2 Pit in the background. They were wooden and were removed in 1909 and 1910. The shaft in the foreground is No. 1. By 1909, more than 90 per cent of the Florence Coal & Iron Company's coal was mechanically cut.

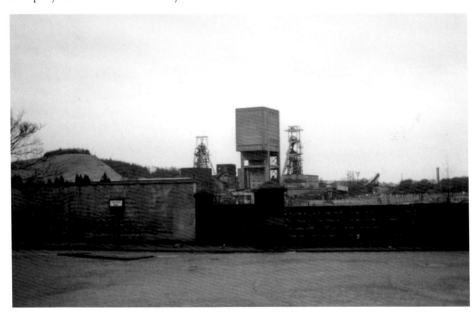

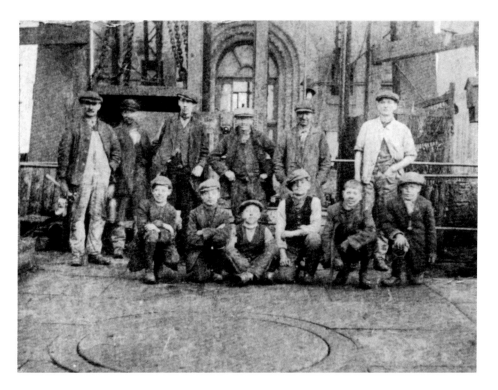

Florence Colliery Employees, Date Unknown, and Florence Colliery, 1994

The pit was worked privately by the Duke of Sutherland until Florence Colliery Coal Ltd was formed in October 1891. This company was dissolved in 1896 and a new one took over operations: the Florence Coal & Iron Company Ltd. From 1911 the pit was run by this company in tandem with the Coking Company Ltd – a subsidiary of Shelton Iron, Steel & Coal Ltd. By 1921, Florence's workforce embraced 1,650 men below ground and 372 men above.

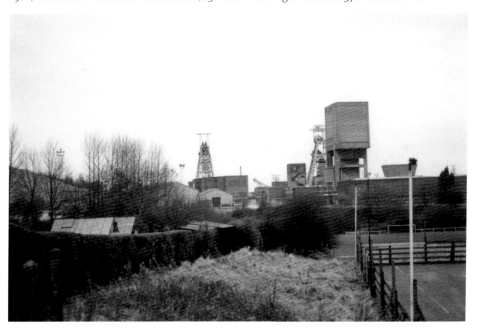

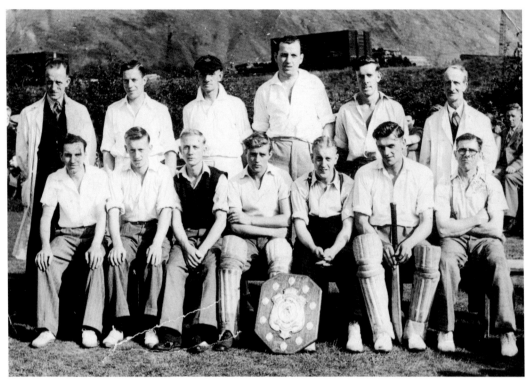

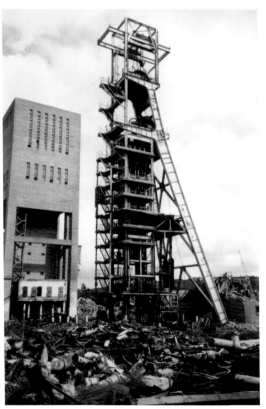

Florence Colliery Fitting Shop Employees, Date Unknown, and Florence Colliery, 1994

The men from the Florence Colliery fitting shops are seen posing in a team group during a colliery knockout tournament. Fourth from the left on the back row is Ken Salt. In 1946, Florence colliers worked the Great Row, Yard, Moss, Rowhurst and Main coal seams. Steam power at the colliery was supplied by twelve Lancashire boilers. The colliery's future prospects looked bright, and it was estimated at the time that it might have a working life of 240 years!

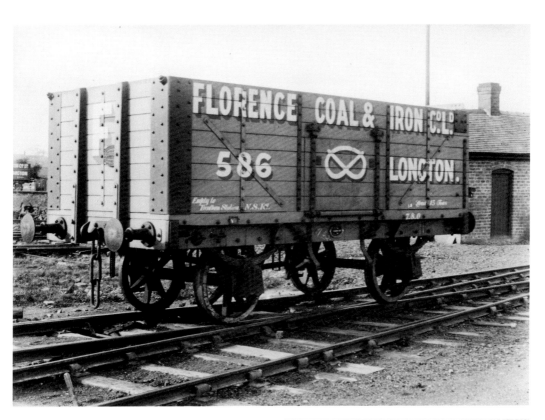

Florence Colliery Railway Truck, Date Unknown, and Florence Colliery, 1994
The colliery's private railway was opened in 1876. It was around 2½ miles in length and linked with the North Staffordshire Railway's main line at Trentham. The 1899 OS map shows the proximity of the private line to the expanding colliery and the adjacent brickworks. By 1914, the pit owned 750 wagons and three locomotives. Locos that saw service at Florence Colliery included *Powerful*, *Bowood*, *Florence* and one called *Terrible*!

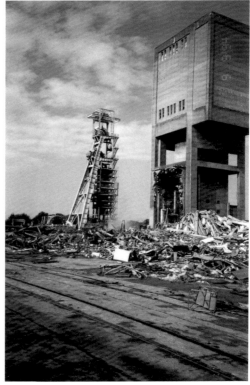

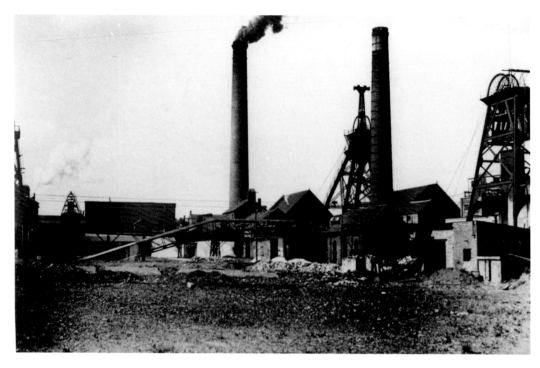

Florence Colliery, Probably Late 1940s, and Demolition of Winding Tower, 1994

The upper photograph would have been taken shortly after the inauguration of the National Coal Board on 1 January 1947. At the time, its assets included 980 coal mines, together with 400 small private mines producing coal under license. Ceremonies at several North Staffordshire collieries marked the event, flags were raised and many events took place in pit canteens. Other collieries in the Longton area at the time of nationalisation were Mossfield and Parkhall.

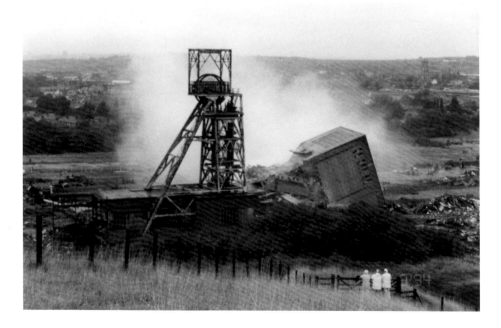

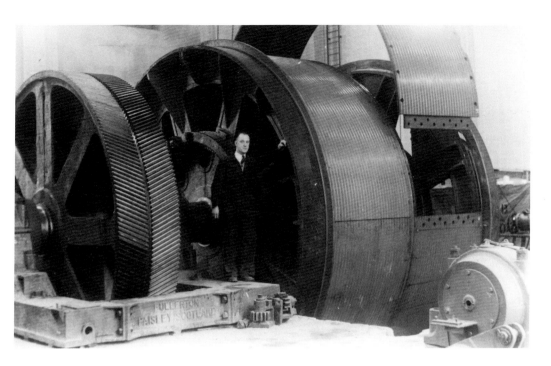

Florence Colliery, Fullerton Electric Winder, 1953, and Demolition of Winding Tower, 1994
The Fullerton electric winder is shown as part of the improvements at Florence in the 1950s. In spite of the modernisation of the colliery, mining remained a dangerous profession. The following miners all died at Florence in this decade: Lawrence Buxton, William Lander, Arthur Shemilt, Frederick Dale, Roy Pendelow, Alfred Clarke, Vincenso Deramo, James Stewart Galloway, Joseph Herod, William James McSparron, Edwin Reid and Antonio Sivoli.

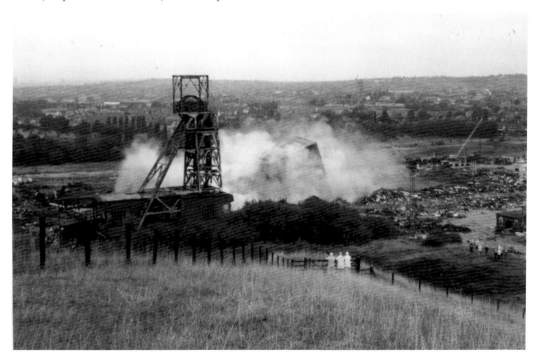

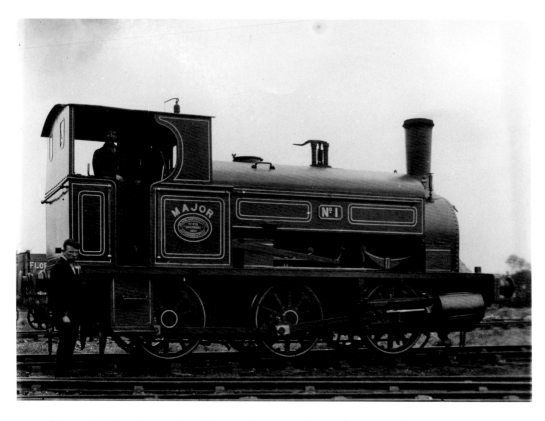

Florence Colliery Locomotive, Date Unknown, and Demolition of Winding Tower, 1994
Major, given the number 972, was built by Black Hawthorn & Company of Gateshead on Tyne and expected to arrive at the pit within nine weeks of the Duke of Sutherland's order of 7 September 1890. This loco was dismantled around 1940 and scrapped around 1942. A new loco shed was constructed of brick in the mid-1950s.

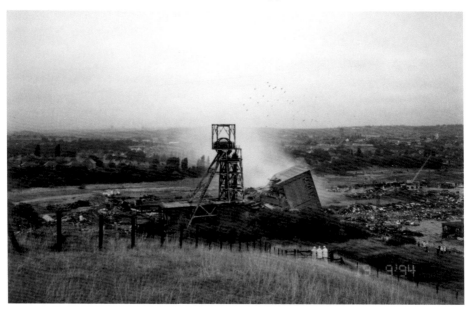

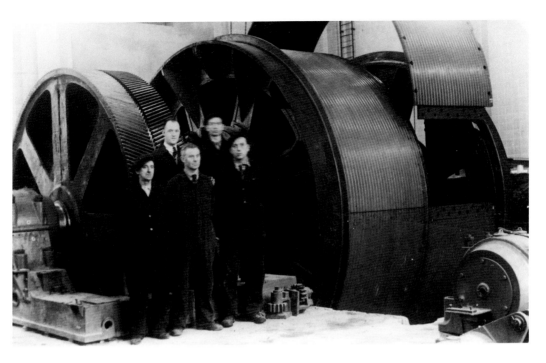

Florence Colliery, Late 1950s, and Demolition of Winding Tower, 1994
Florence Colliery was extensively modernised from the late 1950s; here we see the introduction of electric winders. Tom Pegg is at the front left, while Ken Salt is front right. No. 3 shaft was deepened to 906 yards and Nos 1 and 2 were increased in diameter. All-new surface facilities and a new coal preparation plant were introduced.

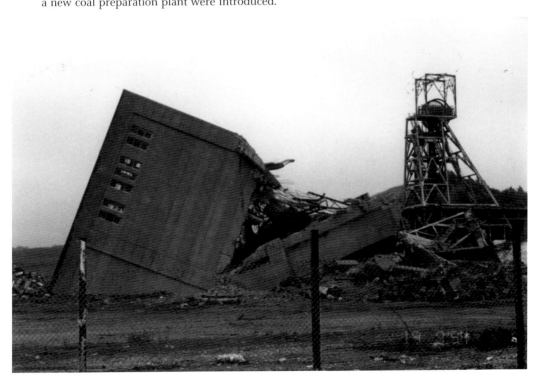

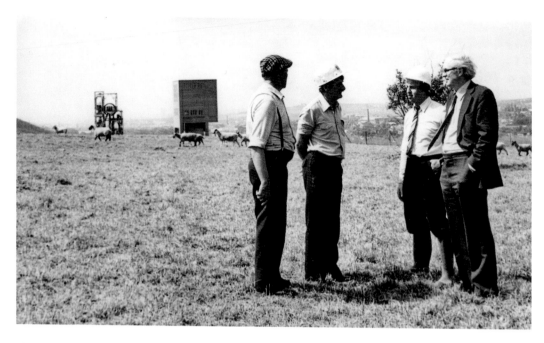

Florence Colliery, 1983, and Site of Three Shafts from Top of Dirt Tip, 2007
The upper photograph shows discussions taking place about the restoration of the colliery tip
into pasture land, for renting out to a local farmer. The figures are: -?-; -?-; Peter Jones, landscape
architect; and Brian Burton, deputy director (administration), Western Area National Coal Board.
Miners at the pit received a newsletter called the 'Florence Fanfare', containing colliery notices
and advice on safety issues as well as jokes and cartoons.

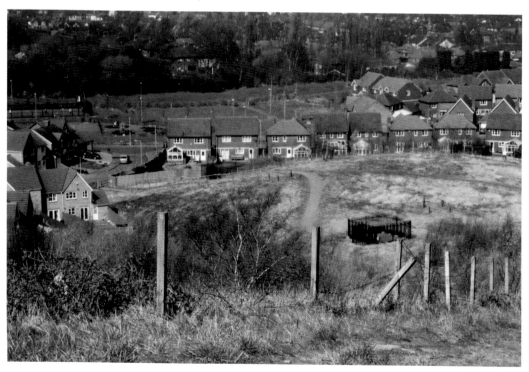

Florence Colliery, Date Unknown, and Site of Former Shaft, 2007

Florence miners were able to enjoy a full social life outside of the pit. They fished at locations such as Knypersley Pool and even organised deep-sea fishing trips off Barmouth. There was also cricket, darts, bowls and the Florence Colliery football club. The Florence Sports & Social Club in Lightwood Road held regular discos. At the end of 2000 it almost faced extinction, with trustees deciding to wind it up. However, the Coal Industry Social Welfare Organisation helped to save the club and reinvented it to welcome the whole community rather than just miners.

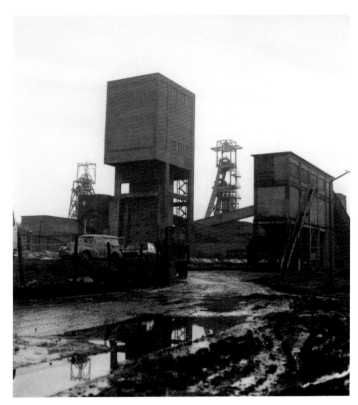

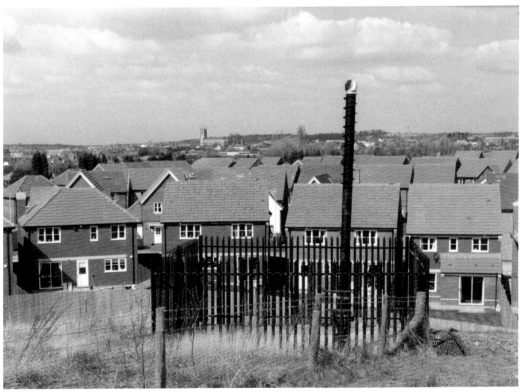

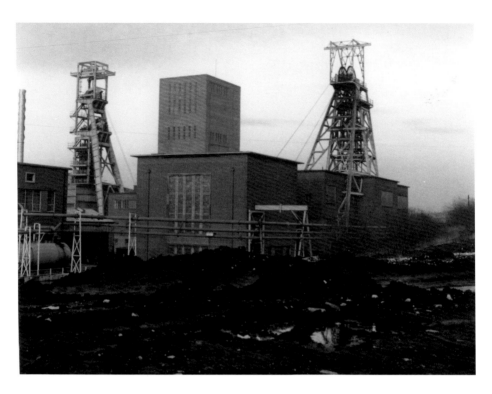

Florence Colliery, Date Unknown, and Site of Former Shafts, 2007

One miner, Harold Tranter, worked at Florence Colliery for almost fifty years, until 1976. In 1974, the National Coal Board announced that the pit was to be connected to its near neighbour, Hem Heath Colliery. The scheme, called the Trentham Project, was completed between 1980 and 1990, an underground link and a new drift being established. The subterranean connection between Florence and Hem Heath was made in April 1979. A classic photograph survives of a group of miners smiling for the camera beneath a sign that states 'you are now entering the Florence section of the mine'. Trentham Superpit closed in 1992, with the loss of 1,400 jobs. It was the last operating coal mine in the Potteries.

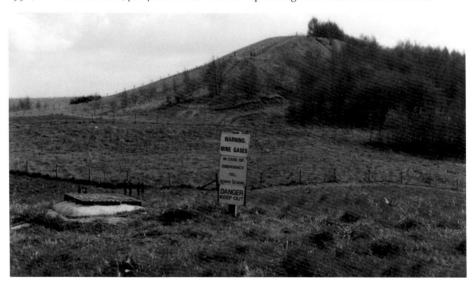

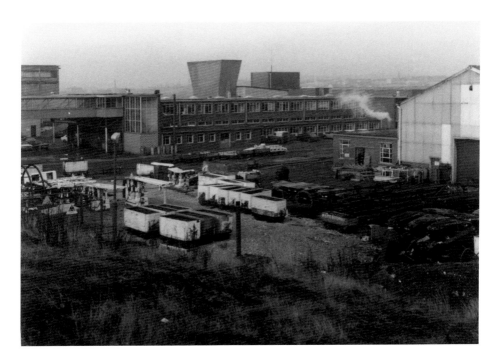

Florence Colliery, Date Unknown, and Site of Former Shafts, 2007

Following the demolition of the Florence complex in 1994, a housing estate and much open space now occupy the old site. In 2006, a 6-foot by 4-foot plaque was unveiled at Florence Colliery Sports & Social Club listing the names of all 101 miners who died from accidents while working at Florence Colliery between 1875 and 1992. The youngest of the listed miners is Charles Parker, aged thirteen, who died in 1913 from terrible injuries after one of his legs caught in a chain and he was pulled into machinery. The oldest was William Lander, aged seventy, who perished in 1953 when an underground wall collapsed on him.

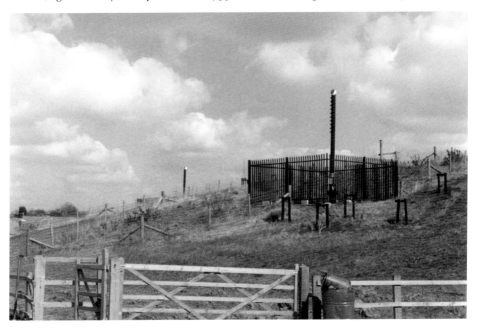

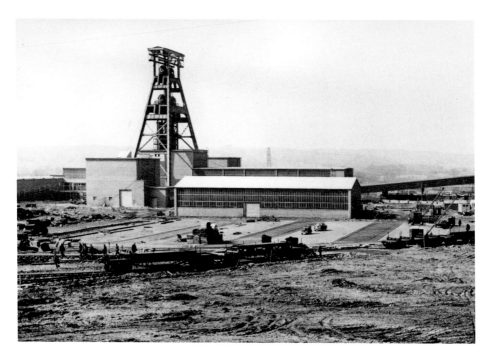

Hem Heath Colliery, 1958, and Colliery and Car Park, 1990s

Hem Heath Colliery was a relatively new pit, the first sod being cut in July 1924 by the Duke of Sutherland, who was then the chairman of the Stafford Coal & Iron Company. The objective was to exploit coal reserves south of the Stafford Colliery in Fenton, as well as the Bassey Mine ironstone. The following photographs relate to the colliery's expansion in the 1950s, when it was completely rebuilt, and are juxtaposed with its final days in the 1990s.

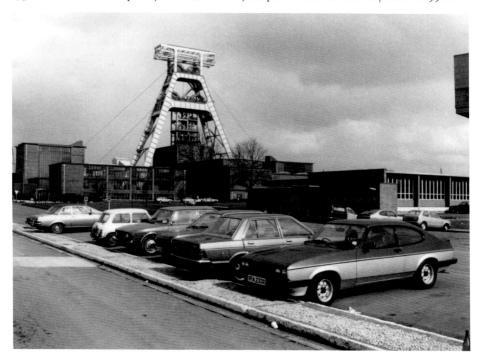

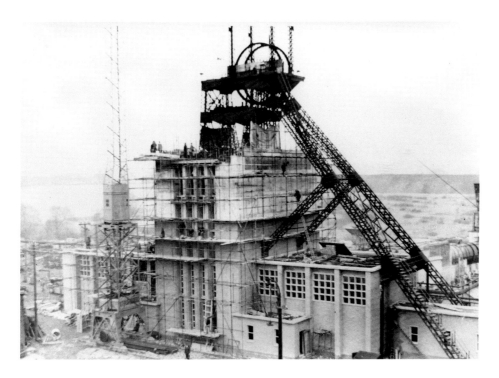

Hem Heath Colliery, Construction of Airlock and Colliery, 1990s
The opening in 1924 was greeted with much optimism. The entrance to the colliery was from the main Trentham to Longton road. Interestingly, the owners accepted that there were concerns about how the new undertaking would 'affect the charm of the picturesque village of Trentham and its environs'. They pointed out that the work and wages provided by the colliery would compensate for any spoliation of the environment. Restructuring occurred from 1950, it being felt that the existing shaft arrangements were inadequate.

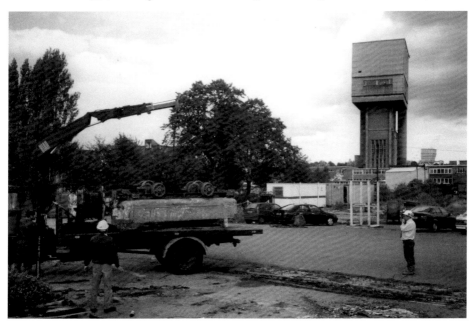

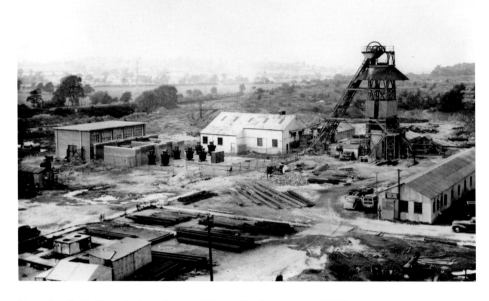

Hem Heath Colliery Substation and No. 2 Shaft, 1953, and 'A' Frame, 1990s
Work began in 1950 on sinking a new shaft (No. 2) which would be 24 feet in diameter
and 1,134 yards deep. It became the third deepest in the country upon its completion in
November 1954. Deepening of the original (No. 1) shaft began in 1956, the depth being
extended to 1,115 yards by December 1957. The objective of the scheme was to increase the
production figure of 243,632 tons in 1950 to 1,250,000 tons by 1963.

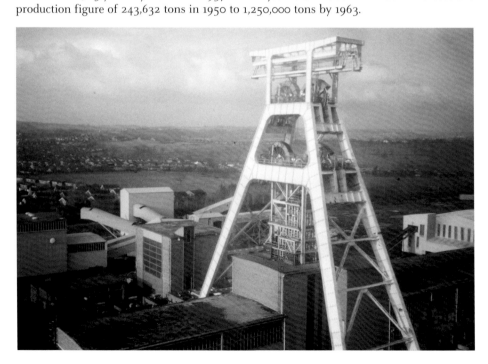

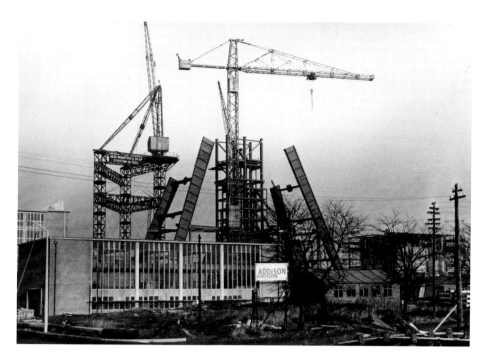

Hem Heath Colliery, 1950s, and Colliery and Keith Meeson, 1990s
The first pithead baths block, including the canteen, was finished by June 1950. The sidings were completed by 1956 and a second pithead baths block was completed by the end of 1956. The main administration block was completed in 1958. Mining historian Keith Meeson, pictured at Hem Heath, has done much to highlight the legacy of North Staffordshire miners. Notable among his achievements has been his championing of a memorial to the Sneyd Pit disaster, which was ultimately erected in Burslem marketplace.

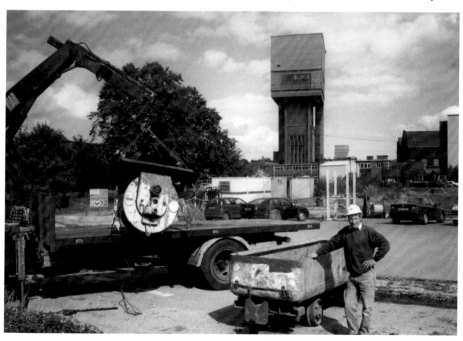

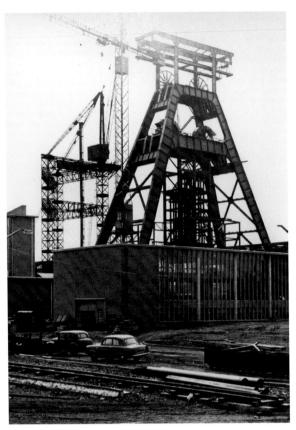

Hem Heath Colliery, 1956, and Demolition, 1990s

Production never stopped at Hem Heath during the transformation of the site, and there was no shortage of labour. With several older pits closing, there were transfers from other coalfields and many miners found themselves coming to Hem Heath. Pictured is the 'Big A' the name of which is taken from its distinctive headgear. It was the dominant feature of the colliery – a 180-foot high steel-girder construction. It was equipped with two winding systems, each operating a pair of three-deck cages carrying a 3-ton mine car on each deck. This was the coal-winding shaft, whereas No. 1 shaft was now used for service and ventilation. An inappropriately blue sky looks down on a toppled pit wheel during site demolition.

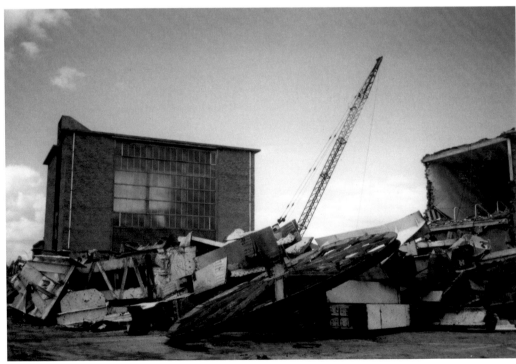

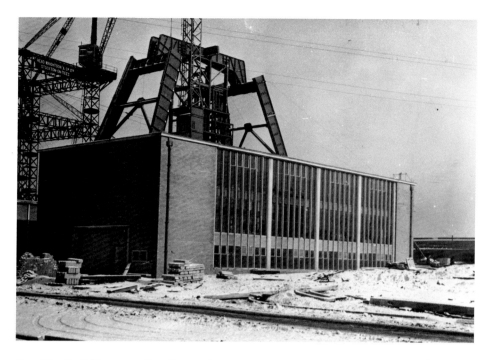

Hem Heath Colliery, 1956, and Demolition, 1990s

Following the underground connection between the Hem Heath and Florence collieries, Trentham Colliery was formed in 1990. Production ceased in 1992, foreshadowing complete closure in 1993. The pit was purchased by Coal Investments Ltd in 1994 and reopened in 1995, before closing once again in May 1996. Afterwards it was returned to the Coal Authority. Demolition soon followed, with the monumental 'A' frame being toppled by explosives experts on 19 August 1997.

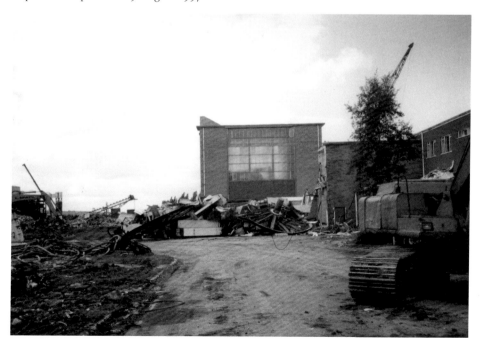

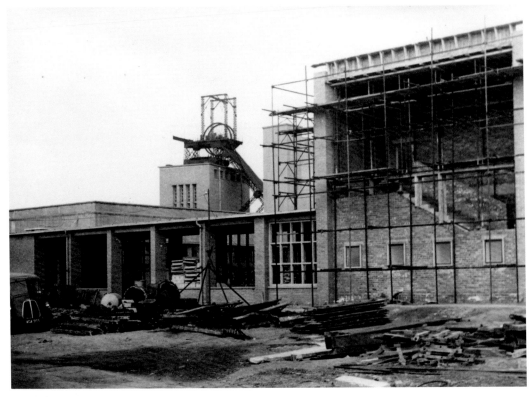

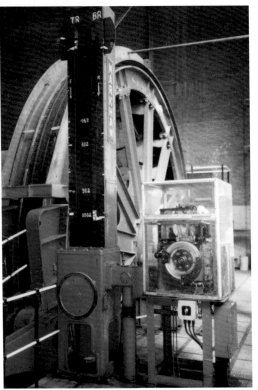

Hem Heath Colliery, Probably 1956, and Winding Engine, 1990s

The parallel drum winder at No. 2 shaft is seen. Its mechanical parts were manufactured and installed by Markham & Co. Ltd. The diameter of the drum was 19 feet 6 inches, the diameter of the rope (winding cable) was 2⅛ inches, and the maximum cable speed was 40 feet per second. No. 2 shaft also incorporated a double-rope friction winder, used for the development of the 912-yard and 1,062-yard pit bottoms, where work began in June 1957 and January 1958 respectively.

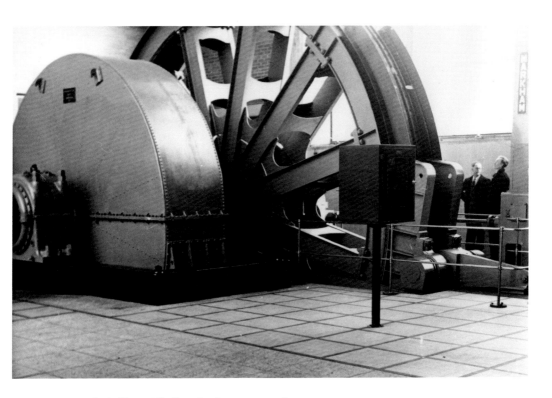

Hem Heath Colliery Winding Engine, 1957 and 1990s

Two more photographs depict the drum winder. The demolition of the 'A' frame that housed it was executed by the Coal Authority without advance public announcement. Angry reactions came from former NUM President John Conan and North Staffs Miners' Wives Action Group member Rose Hunter. Many people believed that the 'A' frame should have been incorporated into site regeneration as a reminder of the city's mining heritage.

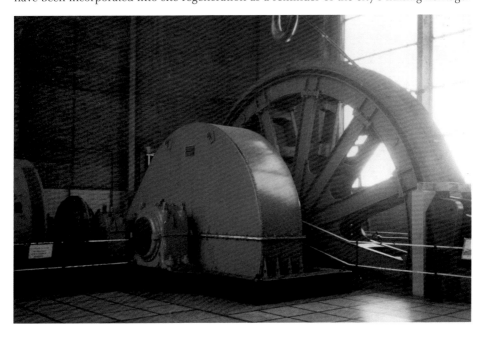

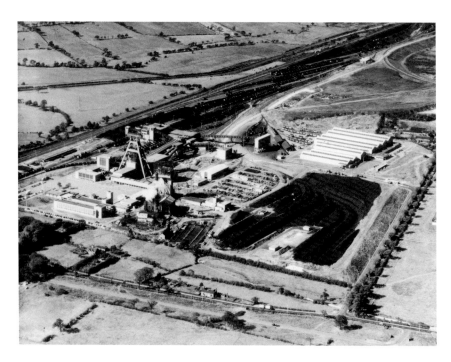

Hem Heath Colliery, 1959, and Hem Heath, Trentham Lakes, 2013
Miners enjoyed much leisure time at Hem Heath Colliery Sports & Social Centre, which replaced the Stafford & Hem Heath Club in Fenton in October 1975. There were even cabaret nights, with appearances from The Searchers and Ken Dodd. The club was surrounded by a cricket pitch, with its own pavilion, scoreboard, and bowling green. In 1985, a designated open day at the pit attracted thousands of interested visitors and the club stayed open for an uninterrupted forty-eight hours.

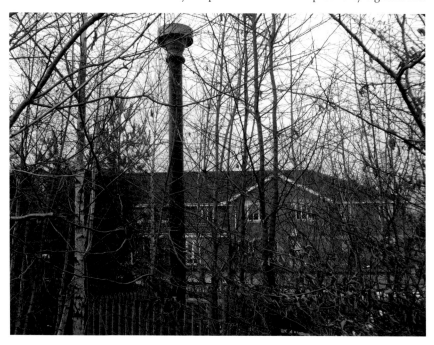

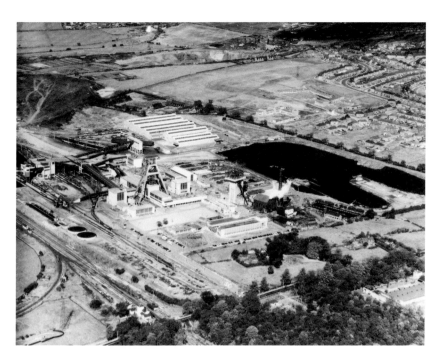

Hem Heath Colliery, 1959, and Donna Louise Hospice, Trentham Lakes, 2013
Derek Prueitt was a miner at Hem Heath from 1967 to 1988. Interviewed by the author of this book, he recalled, 'there was much humour in the pit. We'd drop bags of water from the roadway ceilings on some miners as they passed, or sometimes, we'd take the pit bottom water hoses and spray them at others. Probably they would get their revenge later – but you'd got to be able to take a joke as well as dish it out.'

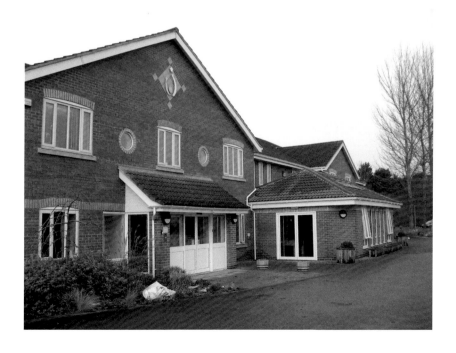

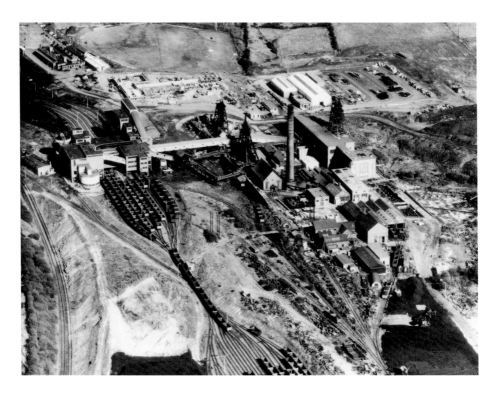

Hem Heath Colliery, 1959, and Donna Louise Trust Fundraisers, 2005

At the time of closure, the colliery could still boast of millions of tons of coal reserves that would have been sufficient to keep the mine in production for decades. Derek Prueitt left the colliery at the age of fifty-two and subsequently landed a job in retail, but was not sentimental about the destruction of the 'A' frame: 'It didn't upset me at all. To me, it was good riddance to an eyesore.'

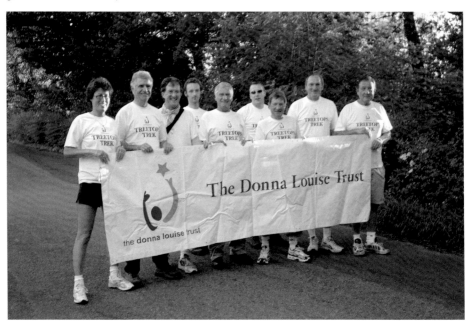

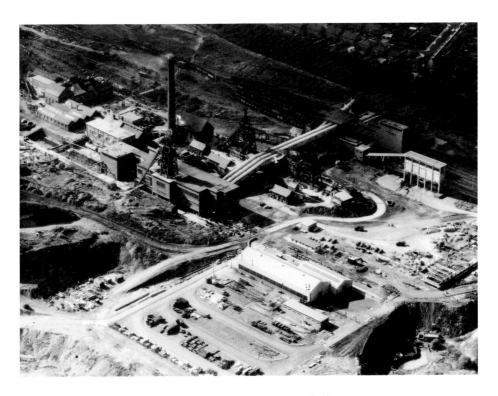

Hem Heath Colliery, 1959, and Donna Louise Trust Fundraisers, 2005
Work began on filling in the shafts at Hem Heath in December 1996, following the site's
return to the Coal Authority. The sprawling old colliery site is now occupied by Trentham
Lakes, a housing and business development. Part of the old site is now occupied by the
Donna Louise Hospice, for whom Keith Meeson (third right) has been a tireless fundraiser.
His sponsored walk of 2005 ended – after 60 miles – at the hospice. The author, fourth
right, accompanied him as pacemaker.

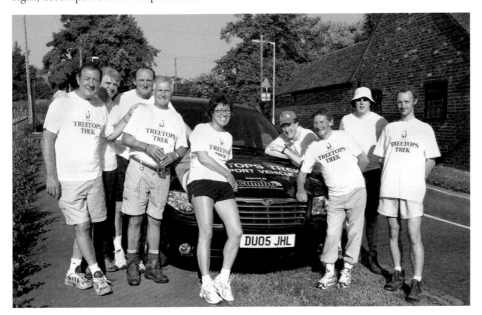

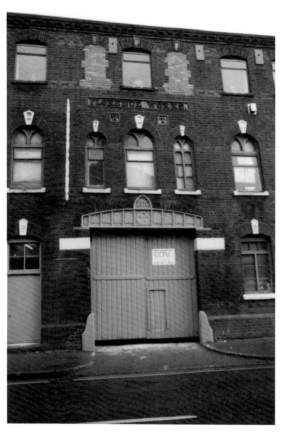

Taylor & Kent's Pottery, and Former Site, 2013

The mining and pottery industries were interdependent in Longton, for the bottle ovens were voracious consumers of coal. J. H. Goddard (1820–83) was both a colliery owner and a pottery exporter. Our next section shows how Longton became known as China Town. As indicated by the date on the façade, the Florence Works of Taylor & Kent, situated on High Street (later Uttoxeter Road), were built in 1876. The works was closed and demolished in the 1990s. All that remains of its frontage are a few courses of brick and the blue-painted iron fenders that were incorporated in the former entrance. The entrance itself has been bricked up.

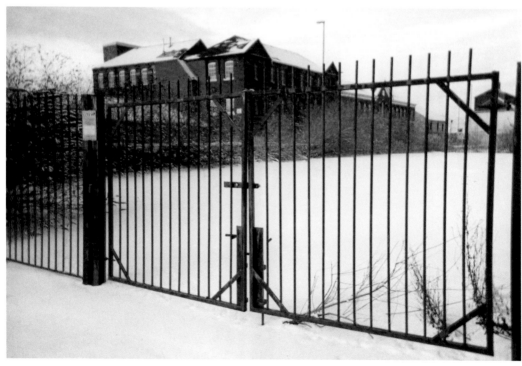

Garfield Works, 1964, and Contour Showers Ltd, Garfield Works, 2013

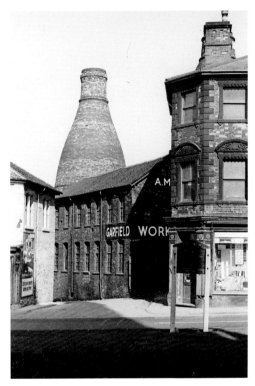

The 1856 OS map, a copy of which can be perused in the Archives Department of Hanley Library, shows the Three Cups beerhouse and an extensive earthenware factory standing directly opposite St James' church on High Street. The *Staffordshire Sentinel* trade directory for 1907 lists 'Jones, Albert E. & Co., earthenware manufacturers, Garfield Pottery'. These 1960s photographs show the Garfield Works standing on the same site, looking from the churchyard. The pottery works was bounded by High Street, Upper Hill Street and Barker Street, now respectively known as Uttoxeter Road, Barlow Street and Barker Street. The Garfield Works, virtually rebuilt, is now occupied by Contour Showers Ltd.

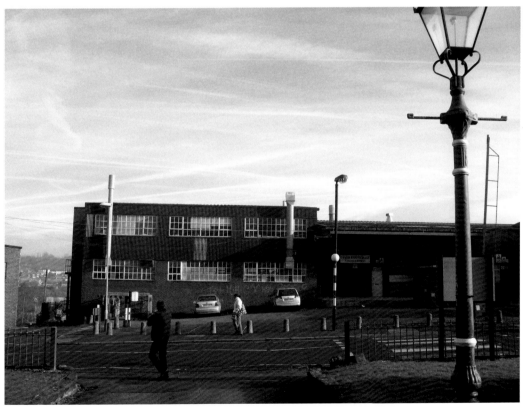

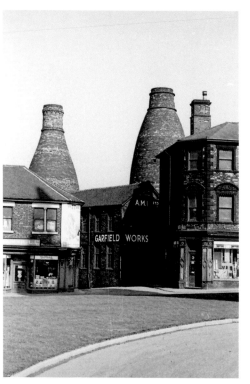

Garfield Works, 1964, and Contour Showers Ltd, Garfield Works, 2013

Uttoxeter Road, a principal communications artery in Longton, was formerly Meer Lane, and is referred to as such on Yates' map of Staffordshire (1775). The town of Longton was then known as Lane End. The map shows that coal and ironstone pits had been established nearby, while later maps show the wealth of industry hugging Uttoxeter Road. Potteries author Arnold Bennett was compelled to record, 'you cannot drink tea out of a tea cup without the aid of the Five Towns. For this the Five Towns is an architecture of ovens and chimneys, for this its atmosphere is as black as its mud; for this it burns and smokes all night, so that Longshaw [Longton] has been compared to Hell.'

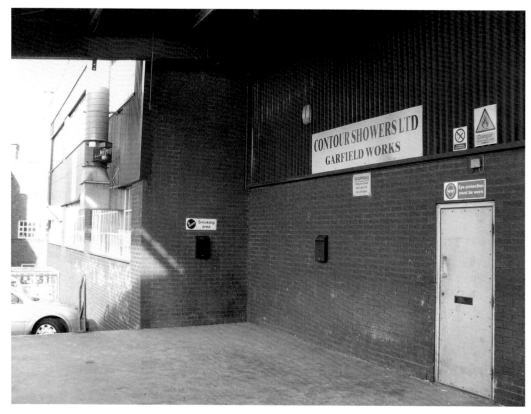

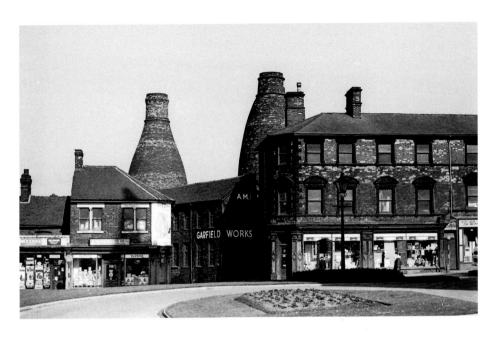

Garfield Works, 1964, and Rear of Factory, 2013

Longton's industrial past has often triggered negative perceptions, and it was not a pretty town. By contrast, the historian Paul Johnson, writing of his childhood in the Potteries in the 1930s, had this to say about 'Neck End': 'I liked Longton, which seemed to me then the most romantic of the six towns [with its] almost perpetual fog spreading mystery through the dingy streets.' Lettering on the rear of the building reminds us of this site's pottery manufacturing past.

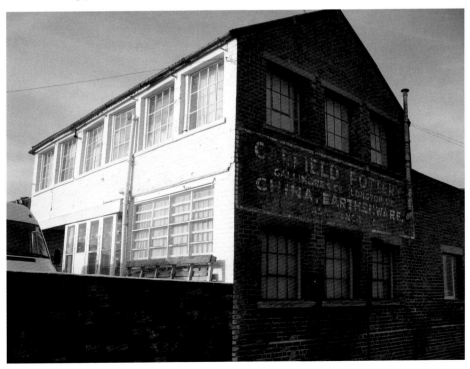

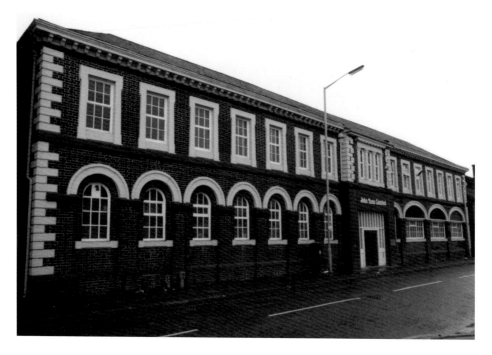

John Tams Pottery, Two Separate Sites, *c.* 1980 and 1997

John Tams was another historic pottery name in Longton, prior to the collapse of the company in 2006. The company had operated the Crown Works in the Strand and also had the Blythe, Sutherland and Atlas Works in Longton. A *Potteries Gazette* advert for 1886 declares that John Tams' Crown Pottery in Stafford Street was producing earthenware for home, colonial and continental markets, 'also to the United States of America'. Items included decorated dinnerware and toilet ware.

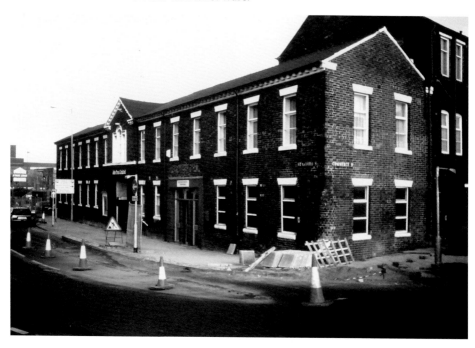

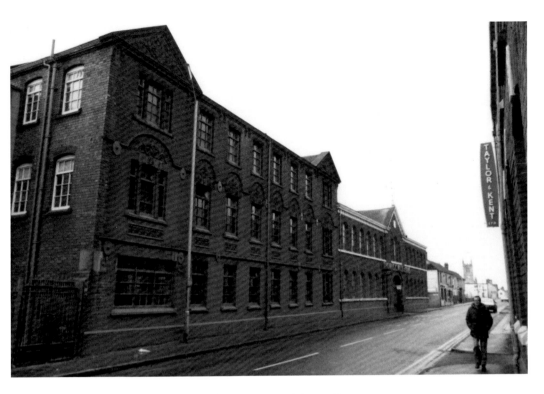

T. C. Wild & Sons, St Mary's Works, *c.* 1980, and Same Site, 2013
Thomas Clarke Wild became the first lord mayor of Stoke in 1928, illustrating the prominence of potters in municipal affairs. He was certainly a key figure in Longton, at one time controlling as many as eleven potteries and also being the owner of the Alhambra Cinema in Normacot. His enterprise as a child was perhaps indicative of much to come: he earned pocket money by carrying water from the local springs to houses in the Normacot area.

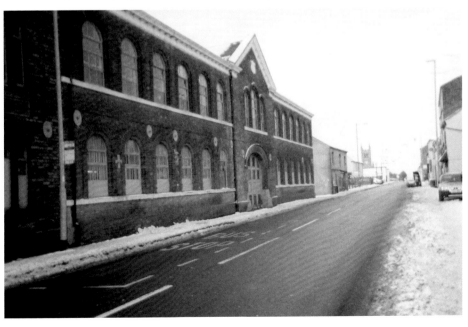

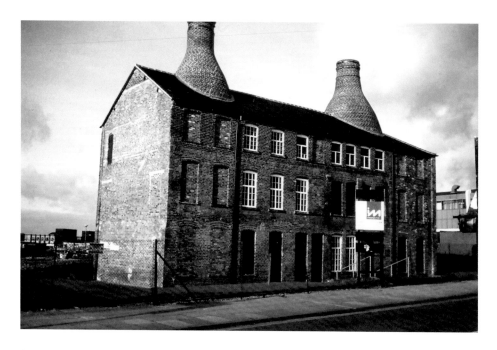

Former Commerce Street Works, 1994 and 2013
Now a Grade II listed building, the premises are shown on the 1877 Ordnance Survey map with the Zion chapel on their right-hand side. The works was in the Chetham family for around half a century, but passed into the hands of Herbert Aynsley & Co. Ltd in 1837. The building is notable for its beautifully symmetrical frontage and for the fact that the bottle ovens are inside the structure.

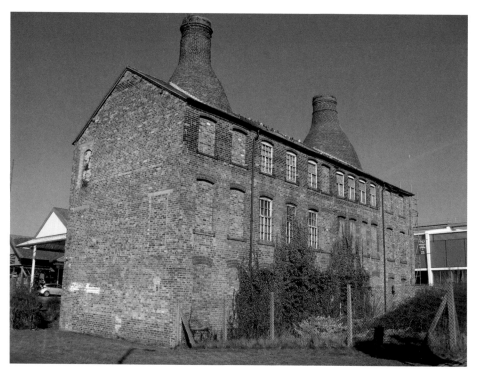

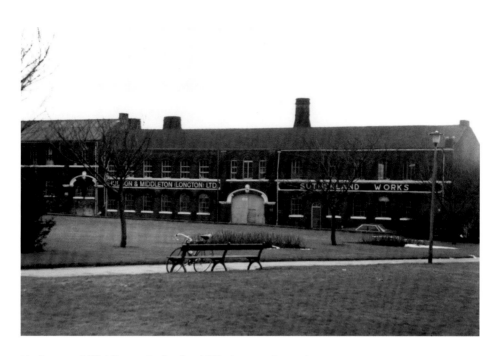

Hudson and Middleton Sutherland Works, *c.* 1980 and 2013

In the 1850s this site was occupied by a brickworks, but by the 1870s a 'china manufactory' had been erected on part of the site. Subsequent rebuilding and extensions created the present factory site. The Hudson and Middleton families were notably involved in producing pottery in Longton, and their histories are separate yet connected. William Hudson Snr was the great-great-grandfather of Graham Birks of Blyth Bridge, whose short history of the family appeared in the *Sentinel* newspaper in 2009.

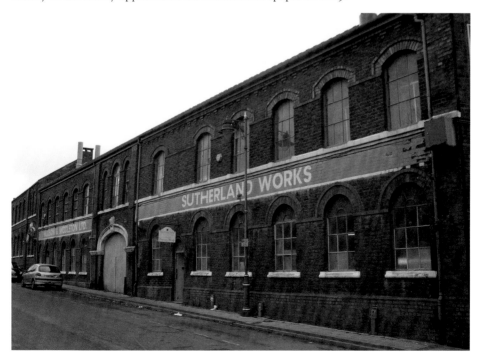

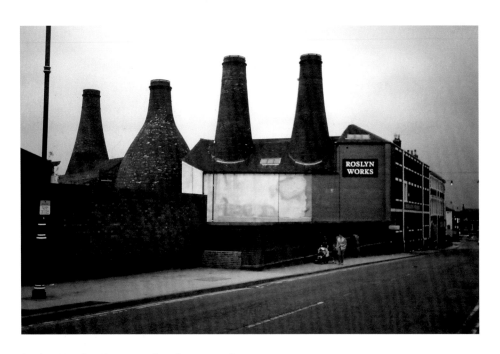

Roslyn Works, Uttoxeter Road, 1997 and 2013
Once known as the Park Place Works, Roslyn is a former pottery works converted into a working museum complex incorporating two bottle ovens. Separate, but not far from the Gladstone site, it was built in the later nineteenth century. A three-storey, twelve-bay frontage incorporates the familiar carriage entrance that gave access to the rear of the premises. It is a Grade II* listed building.

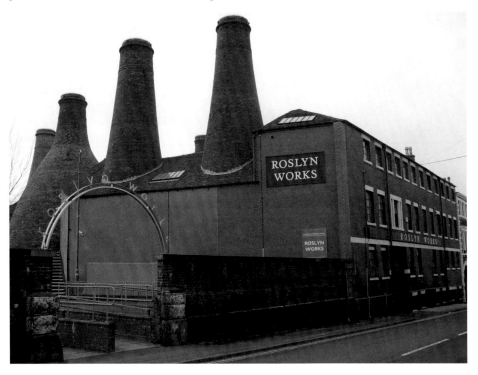

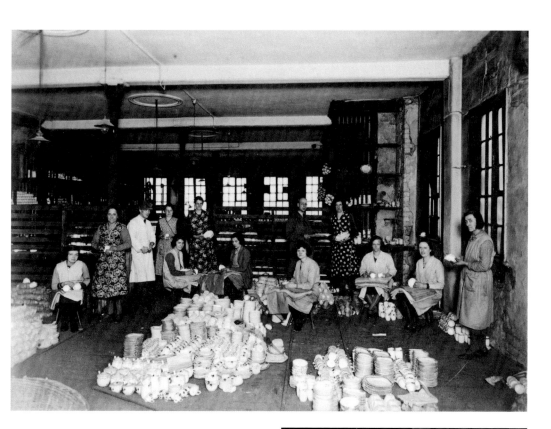

Gladstone China Warehouse, 1930s, and Decorating Shop, 1994

The Gladstone Pottery Museum in Uttoxeter Road is based around the Gladstone Works. The site – whose origins can be traced back to the 1770s – developed piecemeal, like so many others in Longton. By 1840, the factory was described by a government inspector as 'dirty, small, dilapidated and unhealthy'. The present Uttoxeter Road frontage was built in 1856, and the company came to be named after the Victorian Liberal Prime Minister. Some of the employees in the photograph may well have travelled on the company's social excursions. A reproduced notice in the present museum announces the second annual works outing to Rhyl on 24 September 1921. Employees travelled by train from Longton railway station to Rhyl, where they took dinner and tea at Robbins & Sons Café Royal in Queen Street. Staff at the museum, such as the chap in our photograph, Peter Graves, help to interpret traditional potting skills.

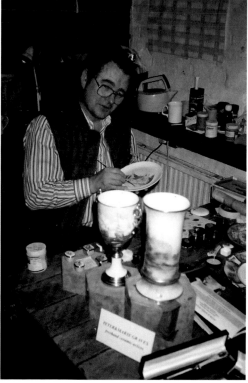

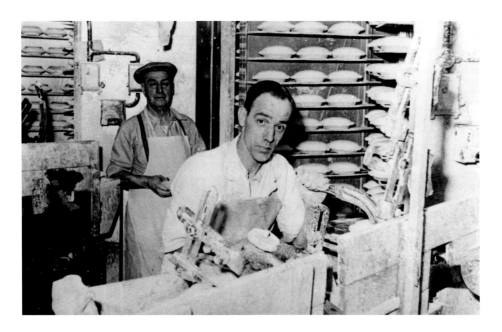

Flat Making, c. 1955, and Rita Floyd, Flower Maker, 2012

Mr Onions is seen on the extreme left of the front row in our top photograph. Most museums rely heavily on enthusiastic volunteers, and this section of the book includes photographs of some from the past and present. Rita, pictured here, worked in the pottery industry for around forty years and can make a china clay flower in less than a minute. Gum arabic is used in this process to make the clay more pliable.

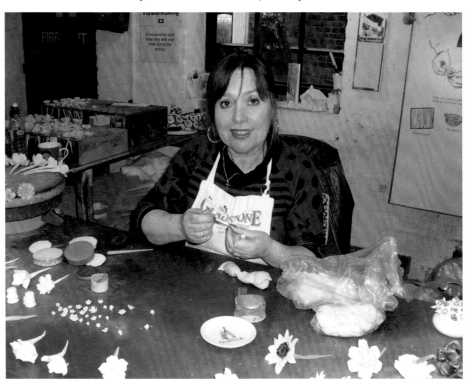

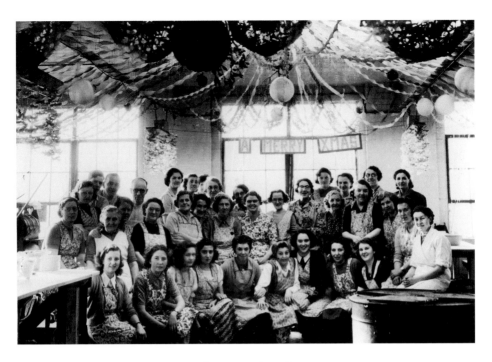

Party in the Factory, Late 1950s, and Kate Davies, Thrower, 2012

Here is a Christmas party or 'fuss' at Thomas Poole & Gladstone China Ltd. Mr Clifford Drury, printer, is next to the man with spectacles. He died in June, 1959. He formerly worked at Wedgwood's Etruria Works and afterwards at the Phoenix Works in Longton. He sometimes printed at Gladstone. Employees kept their 'one and eleven pinnas' on during the 'fuss'. Kate is demonstrating the art of throwing, i.e. making a pot on a potter's wheel.

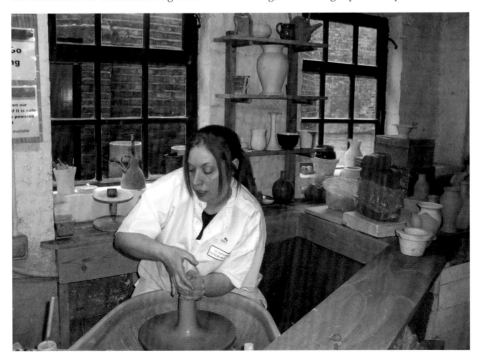

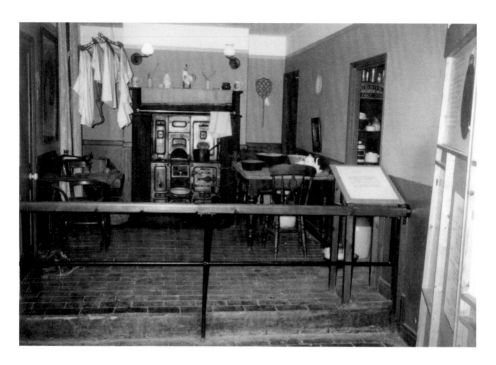

Potter's Cottage, 1991, and Carol Everall, 2013
This display at Gladstone depicts an ordinary potter's terraced cottage, around 1900. Here is the kitchen in what purports to show an improved cottage of the type that was built in Longton from the 1870s. The family lived and ate in the kitchen. There was no bathroom, the toilet being outside in the yard. Carol worked at Coalport in Stoke between 1968 and 1982. She regularly demonstrates her skills as a paintress/decorator at Gladstone.

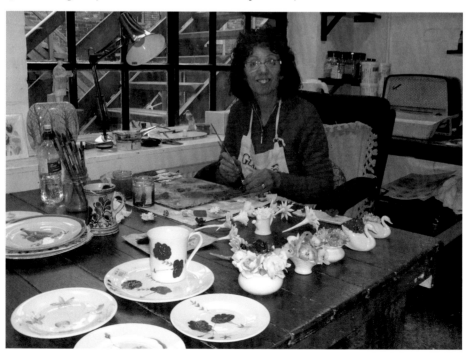

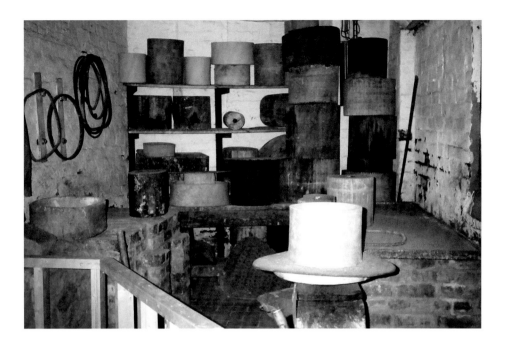

Saggar Maker's Shop, 1994 and 2012

The saggar maker's workshop at Gladstone has changed little over the years. Once the saggars had been made they would be fired once, which means they were biscuit fired, in the same way as house bricks or quarry tiles. Factories needed hundreds of saggars for each firing, though each saggar could be fired about forty times. Stacked up saggars were used as makeshift fences to separate backyards at the rears of terrace houses.

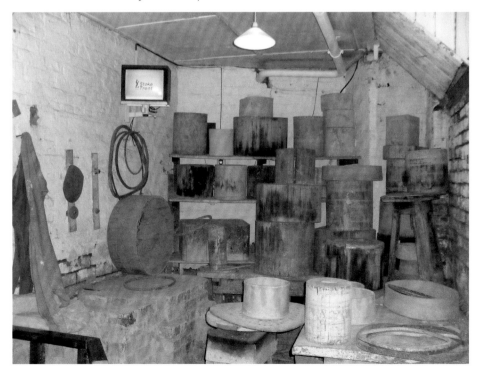

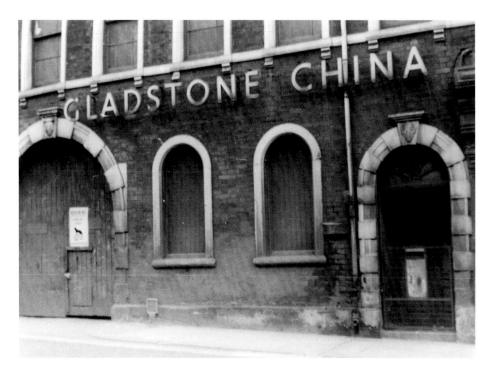

Gladstone Factory Frontage, c. 1971 and 2013

The Uttoxeter Road frontage of the works is shown in an illustration in an 1880s trade directory. The claustrophobic site embraced offices, slip houses, throwing houses, saggar makers' houses and other workshops. Working conditions at this and other factories were horrendous with lead-poisoning and silicosis – known as Potter's Rot – common. Clay dust was an occupational hazard to those working in clay workshops, perhaps brushing and scouring biscuit ware. Consequently, many potters did not live beyond forty.

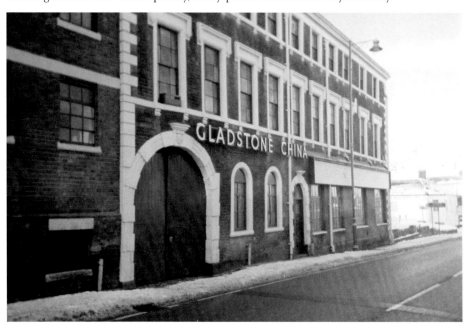

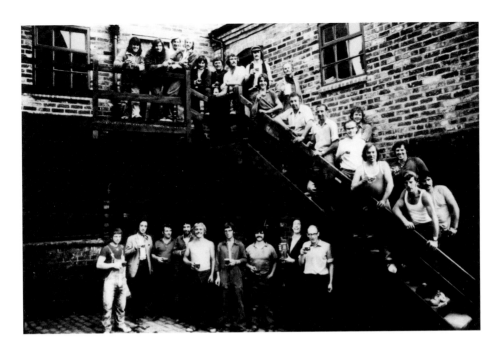

Pre-Restoration, *c.* 1971, and Courtyard, 2013
Builders involved in the restoration of the Gladstone Works, prior to its opening as a museum, pose for the camera. The works faced demolition in 1971 but was saved at the eleventh hour by tile manufacturers H. & R. Johnson. External staircases leading to the workshops are seen in both pictures. They were a factor in the system of segregating workers, while also offering management good opportunities of monitoring the activities of the workers.

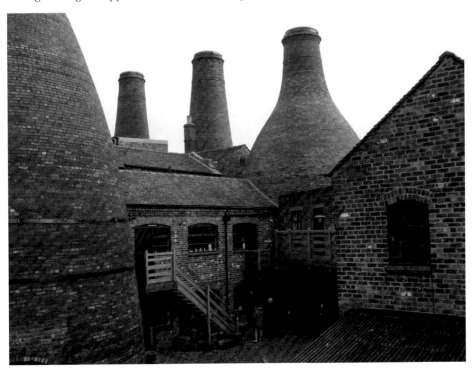

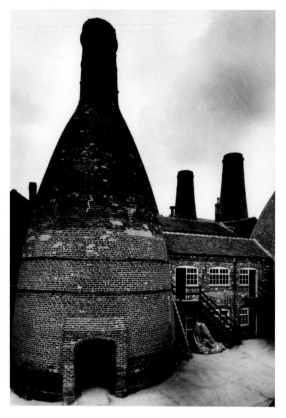

Courtyard, 1973/74 and 2013

The cobbled courtyard at Gladstone reeks of nostalgia, but for the workers who traversed it during the factory's working life, it must almost have been a prison. They worked long hours in order to meet delivery schedules, yet at slacker periods there was no work available. Even in the 1900s, some pottery manufacturers were deducting money from workers' wages for essentials such as tools, machinery, light and water. Lateness, drunkenness and swearing was also penalised by fines. Child labour was at one time the norm, and the present museum quotes the memories of a former boy attendant who worked with a jiggerer: 'I used to have to be there at six in the morning – get two buckets of clean water – clean all the jigger head out and fetch two rolls of clay up, and sometimes after I'd done all this, he wouldn't be there – he'd still be in bed, he'd be drunk over night. So I had to go and fetch him out then, otherwise I didn't get no pay for that day, after I'd done all that.' The upper photograph was taken shortly after the Staffordshire Pottery Industry Preservation Trust was inaugurated in 1971 to restore and run the museum. It was officially opened on 24 April 1975 and subsequently won several awards, including the Come To Britain Trophy (1975), the Museum of the Year (1976) and the Business & Industry Award (1976). Restoration of the site has never really ceased. In January 2012 the *Sentinel* newspaper reported that renovation work on three of the bottle ovens had begun, funded by Stoke-on-Trent City Council and English Heritage.

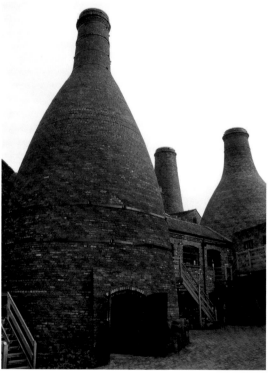

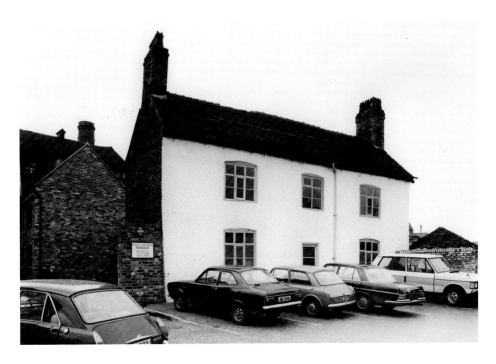

White House, c. 1975 and 2013
From 1952, the factory was under the control of Thomas Poole & Gladstone China, which subsequently bought adjacent properties in the form of the White House and the Vulcan pub with a view to site extensions. However, the decision was ultimately made to concentrate on the existing site. The building, on the Uttoxeter Road and Chadwick Street junction, is now used a storeroom and offices.

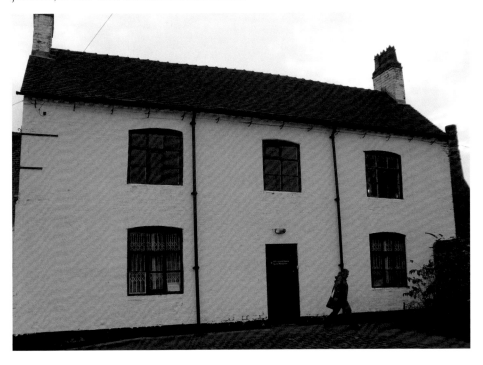

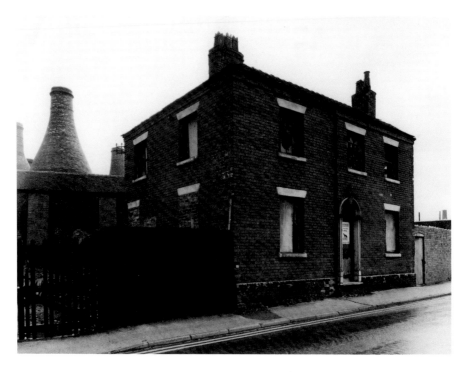

Red House, c. 1975 and 2013

This Chadwick Street building, dating from around 1840, is another feature of the museum site and, like the White House, was statutorily listed in 1993. At one time it accommodated a small pottery-making unit. It is now used by the museum as the Doctor's House and offers an insight into the hazards of working in the pottery industry.

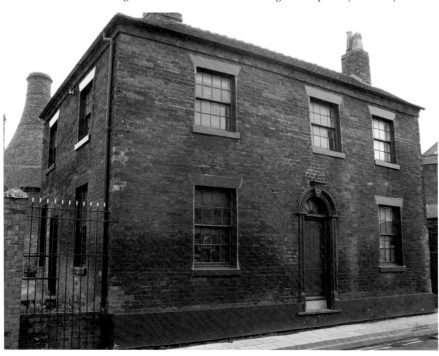

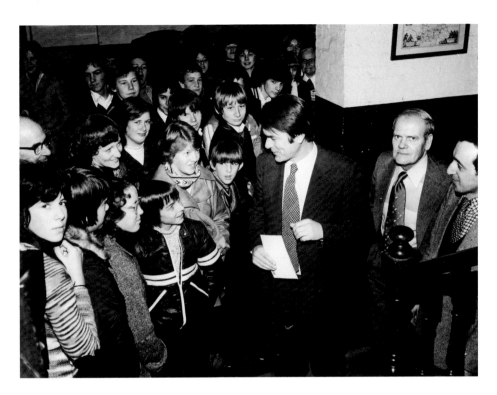

Visit of David Owen MP, 1978, and Tunnel and Lodge, 2012

Gladstone has welcomed many famous visitors over the years, including David Owen MP, as seen here. Of course, he would not have had to 'clock on' as the factory workers used to. At most potbanks, it was the practice for latecomers to be 'gated' or locked out. Starting time for Gladstone workers was 7.30 a.m., with the lodge-keeper shutting the gates ten minutes afterwards. You could not then clock on until 9.30 a.m., losing two hours' work.

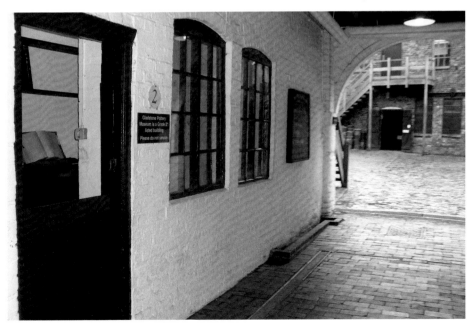

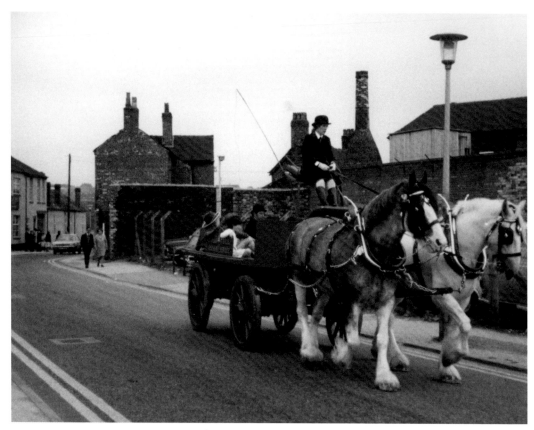

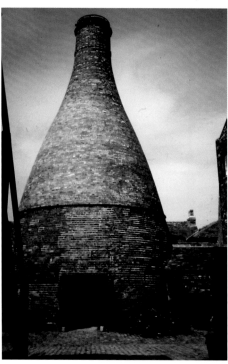

**Last Firing and Dray, 1978, and
Bottle Oven, 1995**

The last firing of a bottle oven with coal took
place at the nearby Sutherland Works in
1978 and was organised by Gladstone Pottery
Museum with special permission being granted
to fire a kiln full of ware. A special film of the
event, narrated by actor Frank Windsor, was
made, entitled *Echoes of A Saggar Maker's
Bottom Knocker – a Bygones Special*. The
commentary described the authentic detail that
went into the occasion: 'Even the fuel arrived
by horse-drawn wagon – though perhaps not
many ladies in bowler hats made the deliveries
in the old days. Certainly, in spite of the coal
dust and the sacks and the smutty atmosphere,
the carts were always kept gaily painted in
bright colours. With three coal mines close by,
there was no energy crisis on this occasion. The
National Coal Board provided their best coal for
free – all 11½ tons of it.'

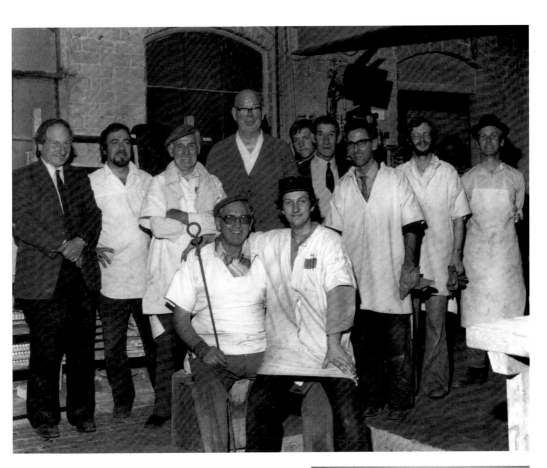

Last Firing Volunteers, 1978, and Flatware, 1995
The volunteers pictured on this historic occasion
are, from left to right: Doctor Celoria, Elwen
James, Ted Lockett, Alf Clough, -?- (a student), -?-,
Fred Greasley, -?-, -?-. Sitting are Les Dennis and
Terry Woolliscroft. Interest in this event helped
Gladstone to achieve its best-ever visitor figures
in 1978, with 80,000 people passing through its
doors. In the lower photograph, a saggar has been
broken to show how flatware is stacked inside.

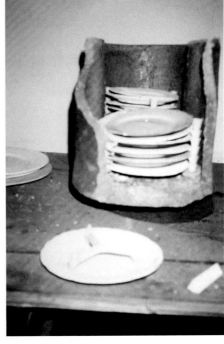

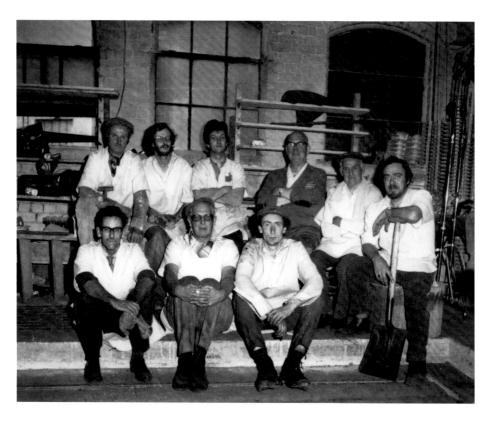

Last Firing Volunteers, 1978, and Thrower, 1994

Here is another photograph of the volunteers at the last firing. Third at the back is Terry Woolliscroft. First on the front row is Fred Greasley, and second along is Paul Niblett. Alf Clough is at the rear in the cardigan. A young demonstrator shows how to throw a pot in the 1994 photograph. Readers may remember an episode of Bruce Forsyth's *Generation Game* in which contestants were asked to try their hands at doing the same.

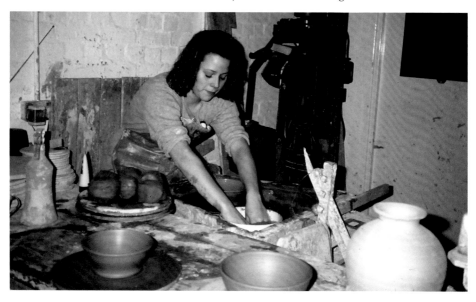

Big Alf, 1978, and Saggars, 1994

Alf Clough's expertise was required at the last firing, which revived the age-old tradition of placing saggars of ware in the oven for firing, bricking up its door and then removing the saggars once they had been fired. The saggar was a fireclay container that protected the ware from the flames and smoke inside the oven. On average, a saggar might survive forty firings. The walls of a saggar were made by wrapping a sheet of clay around a wooden drum. Another lump of clay would be flattened into a shape made by an iron hoop by an assistant using a 'mawl' or mallet. This was the base, made by the employee known as the saggar maker's bottom knocker.

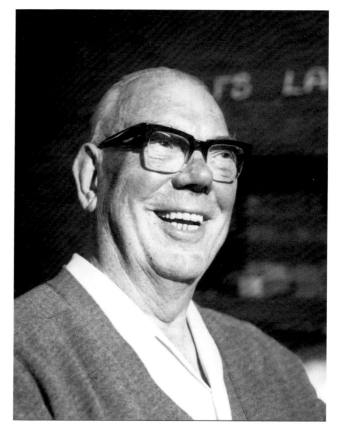

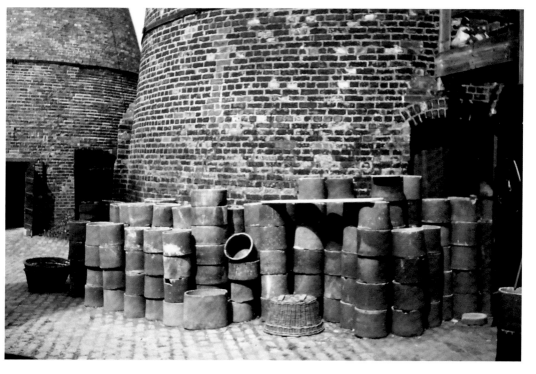

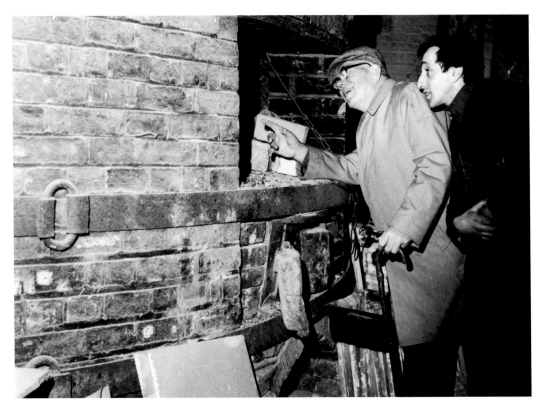

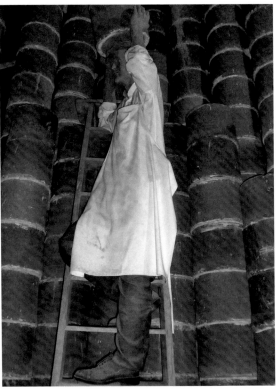

Last Firing, 1978, and Cod Placer, 2012

Our top photograph shows Big Alf and Museum Director David Sekers at the time of the last firing. The model of a cod placer stacking the saggars on his 'hoss' recalls an important part of the entire process. The saggars, once ready for firing, would be passed down a line of men – known as placers – to the cod (or head) placer on his ladder. The saggars would then be stacked in columns, or 'bungs'. We are looking at the cod-placer through the entrance to the kiln, which was known as the 'clammins' or 'wicket'. This was sealed with bricks and mortar before firing. The outer rings of saggars would be those that were most heat-resistant, as they were nearest to the firemouths. Time was money on potbanks, and so the bricked clammins would often be knocked down and the fired wares taken out while they were still hot, exposing workers to extreme heat.

Last Firing, 1978 and Flower Maker Frances Hall, 1994

Smiling for the camera at the time of the last firing are Paul Niblett, Kathy Niblett (*née* Woolliscroft) and Terry Woolliscroft. Museum staff and volunteers are very patient in explaining their various skills to visitors in the Making Shops. The flower-making demonstrators lubricate their hands with olive oil to prevent the clay from sticking to their skin. Small pieces of textured wood create patterns on the clay in imitation of the veins of petals or leaves. Other tools are used to create a stippled effect. Dried flowers are biscuit fired, making them hard and white, and then fired again with a clear glaze. They are then hand-painted with enamel colours and fired for a third time. The flower makers at Gladstone can make over forty different bone china flowers.

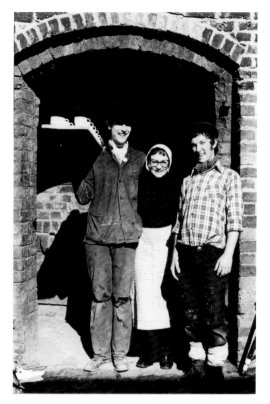

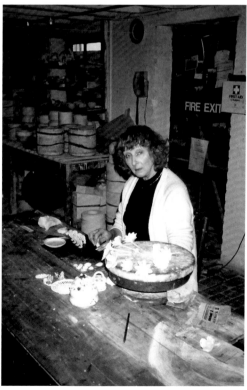

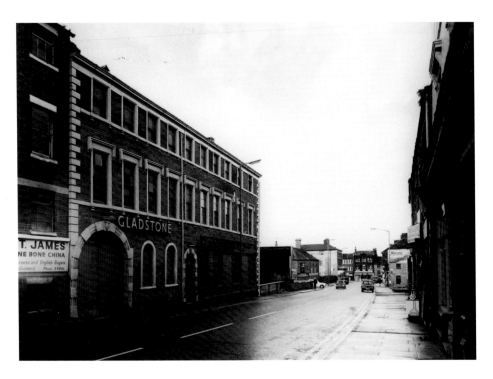

Gladstone and Uttoxeter Road, *c.* 1978, and Courtyard in Snow, 2013
The *Bygones Special* television programme was concluded with footage of amused visitors watching the volunteers smashing up the saggars that had carried the ware during the last firing. The top photograph was taken roughly at the time of the last firing and shows the impressive factory frontage of Gladstone. Elegant, symmetrical façades such as this often hid frenetic industrial activity and the unhealthy working conditions behind them. The Vulcan pub formerly stood immediately to its right.

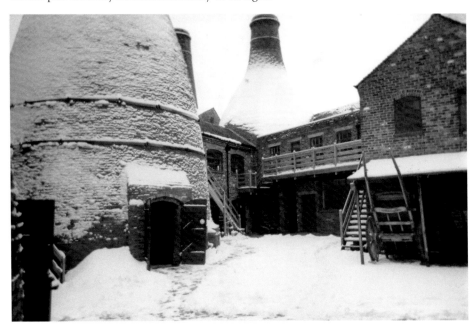

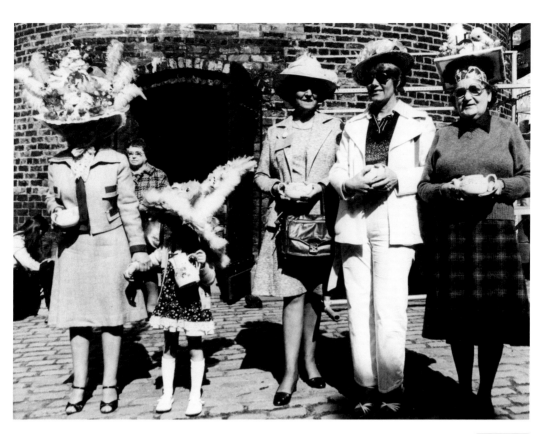

Museum Easter Bonnet Parade, Probably Late 1970s, and Paul Niblett, 2013

Events at Gladstone have been plentiful over the years, while the museum's evocative surroundings have also attracted the television cameras on many occasions, with the series *Most Haunted* having filmed here. Volunteer Paul Niblett was one of a group of engineering volunteers from the Institution of Mechanical Engineers who were looking for a project to work on in the early 1970s. They joined Gladstone and met the volunteers already on site. Paul explains, 'My friends and I soon realised that as skilled engineers there were specific areas where we could help – one of which was to recreate the slip house and the engine house. We began coming along on Thursday nights in late 1971, and we've been coming along ever since. There are three of us left from those very early days. We'll paint, clean drains, oil machinery, or turn our hands to anything urgent.'

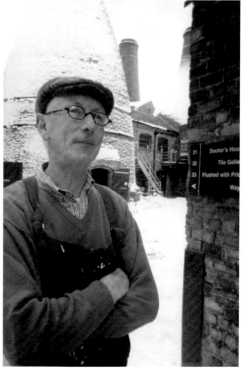

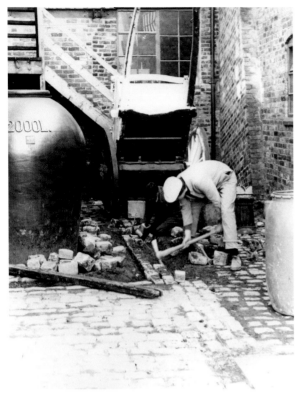

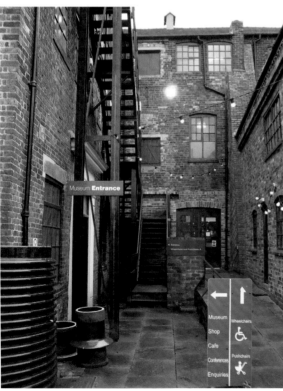

Museum Entrance, 1981 and 2012
Here is the cobbled approach to the museum, also our means of exit. The visitor centre that is accessed from here was officially opened in July 1995. This and other improvements were funded by European money via the Ceramic Design Quarter Urban Pilot Project. Much renovation work was done on the site's bottle ovens in 2012, with the museum thankfully remaining open. On 8 December 2012, a Dickens Day was held in order to celebrate the 200th anniversary of the author's death. Regular events at Gladstone still flourish, such as 'Meet Miss Byrne'; an actress, speaking in character, appears as a factory inspector in the 1910 office. Today, the museum is nationally acclaimed and internationally recognised as one of the premier industrial heritage sites in Europe. Present museum manager Angela Lee – who first worked as a volunteer at Gladstone in the 1980s – attempts to explain the ongoing fascination of the museum: 'Regular visitor questions concern the height of the bottle ovens. They're about 60 feet, but they're all different from each other. I'm also asked how many people worked at Gladstone in its working heyday. It was about a hundred.' One postscript to our section on the pottery industry: in January 2013, the *Sentinel* reported that Clara Middleton had just celebrated her 106th birthday and was thought to be the Potteries' oldest resident. During her working life she was employed at a number of pottery companies, including Thomas Poole & Gladstone China Ltd.

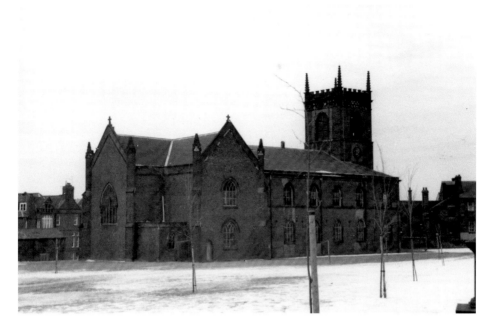

St John's Church, 1970s, and Former Churchyard, 2013

We now feature some ecclesiastical buildings. The church of St John the Baptist was consecrated in 1764. It was funded by public subscriptions, including a large endowment from John Bourne, the town clerk of Newcastle-under-Lyme. It was registered as a chapel for Protestant dissenters, though Church of England services took place there. The rapid increase in Longton's population – as well as the church's poor state of repair – led to its demolition. It was replaced by the church we see here, consecrated in 1795.

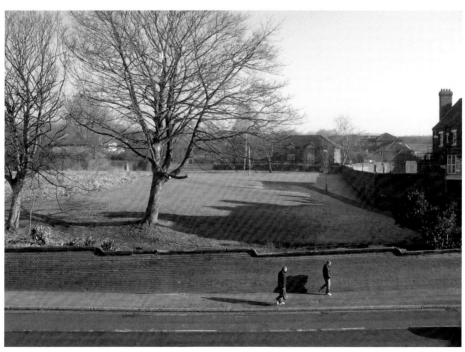

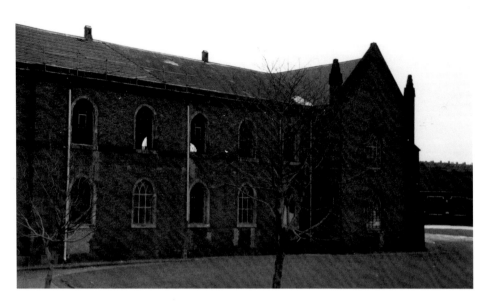

St John's Church, 1970s, and Former Churchyard, 2013

There were improvements made to the church in the nineteenth century. In 1816 a clock was installed in the tower. In 1827/28 the east end of the church underwent extension and a stone-embattled parapet was added in 1832–34, to the design of T. Johnson. John Ward wrote, around 1840, that St John's would seat about 1,200 persons. At the time, its attached cemetery covered 2½ acres.

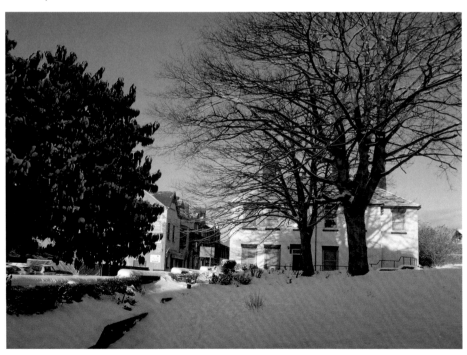

St John's Church, 1970s, and Former Churchyard, 2013

Some of us stray from the path of righteousness. In 1856, the following report appeared in the local press: 'A Drunken Preacher: We learn that at Longton Church, on Sunday last, a newly-imported curate, who was to have preached a funeral sermon, was suddenly taken sick in the early part of the morning's services; some of the people supposed through the previous night's debauch; and after vomiting a quantity of filth, had to be taken from the church, and was led home, being jeered at by the boys as he passed through the streets. We hear the congregation, *en masse*, left the church, and his anti-teetotal Reverence has not since been heard of in the locality.'

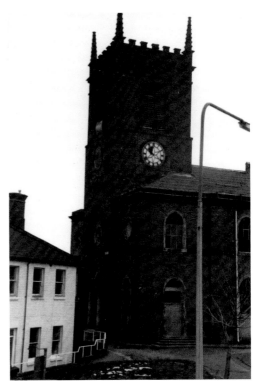

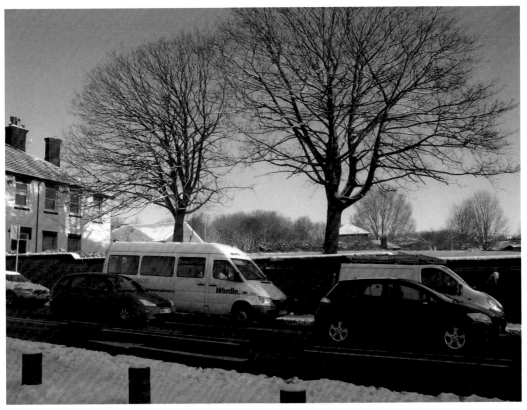

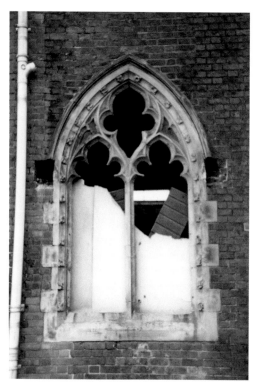

**St John's Church Window, 1970s,
and Former Churchyard, 2013**

St John's graveyard was presenting the
neighbouring hotel with problems by 1850:
'At the 'Crown and Anchor', the cellars
receive a drainage of the churchyard, and
cannot be used. The churchyard is above the
general level of the street, and close to the
road...' It was also the case that potters' waste
was often dumped in the churchyard, leading
to graves being dug into the mix of soil and
potters' refuse. The difficulty of burying
the dead can be seen by the fact that boring
rods were sometimes used to ascertain
whether grave plots had been used in recent
years. The subsidence-damaged church was
demolished in the late 1970s.

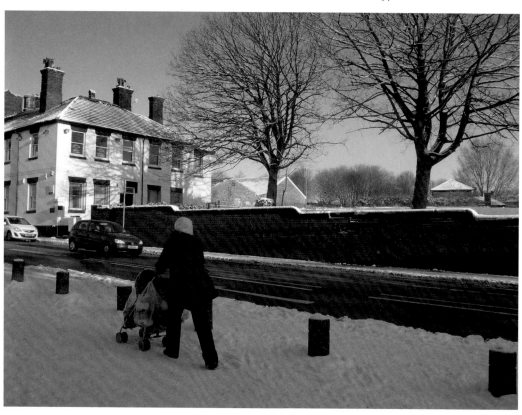

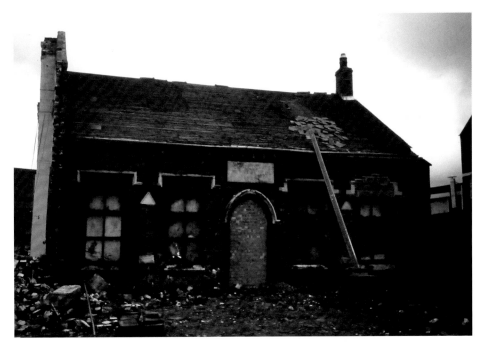

St John's Infants' School Demolition, 1994, and Former Churchyard, 2013

Church of England schools were prominent in educating the masses in Stoke-on-Trent from 1815. National schools were built in Stoke (1815), Hanley (1816) and Burslem (1817) before one was erected in Longton in 1822. The infants' section was added in 1829, on the right-hand side of the main block, and we see it here in the course of demolition.

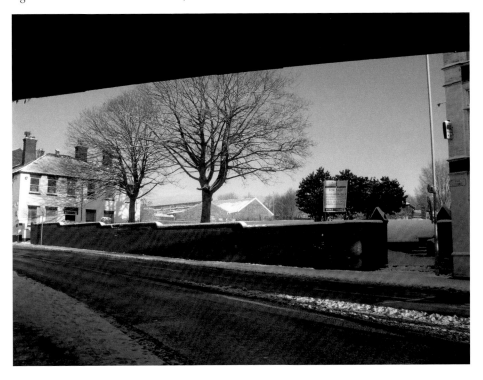

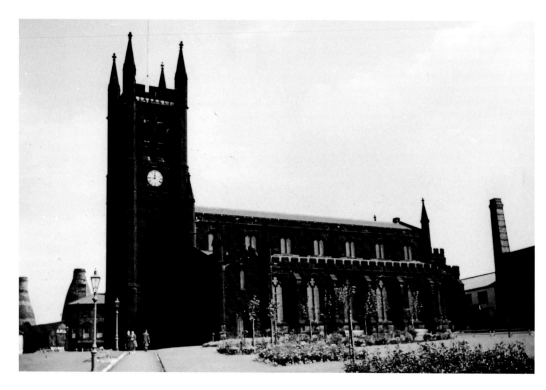

St James's Church, Probably 1950s and 1994

With St John's church struggling to accommodate a growing population, another Anglican church was built in High Street. St James's, designed by James Trubshaw and consecrated in 1834, was made the parish church when Longton became a parish in 1839. St John's continued as a chapel of ease until 1866 when there was a review of parish boundaries and the parish of St John the Baptist, Lane End, was created.

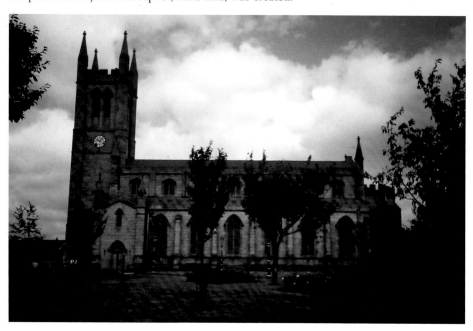

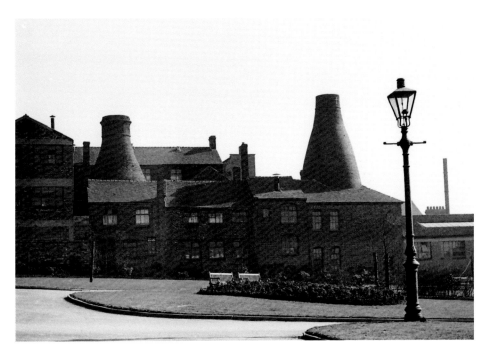

Different Views from Around St James's Church, *c.* 1964 and 2013

St James's church was designed in the Perpendicular style with a 90-foot tower surmounted by four pinnacles. It had room for 2,000 worshippers, but never attracted anywhere near this number. The church served an industrial town and was surrounded by factories, as both our pictures show. Insalubrious working and living conditions in Longton led to a high mortality rate, which soon filled the churchyard and blackened the beautiful Hollington stone of St James.

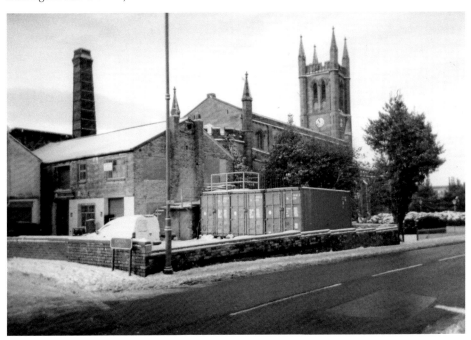

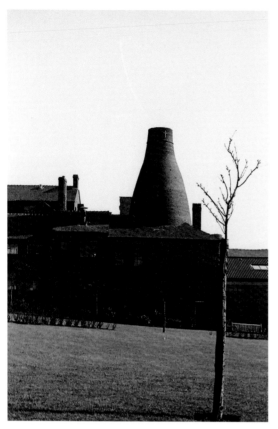

Different Views from Around St James's Church, c. 1964 and 2013
The churchyard was landscaped and laid out as gardens in 1960. The removal of large quantities of soil and grass was required, much of which had been rendered infertile by the soot-filled atmosphere of industrial Longton. The cost of urgent repairs led to fears that the church might have to be demolished in the 1980s, but church funds and a grant from the city council enabled a restoration programme to begin in 1993. Ongoing work – and additional funding from the National Lottery, English Heritage and the Historic Churches Trust – allowed further work to be completed by January 2003. The entire church was made weatherproof and the tower re-pointed. The bottom picture was taken from Normacot Road.

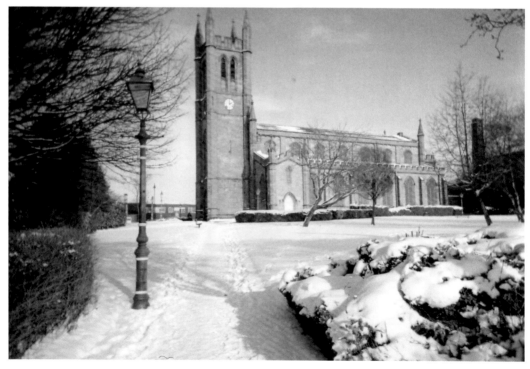

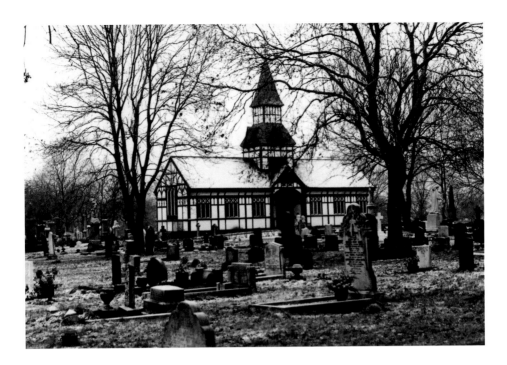

Longton Cemetery Chapel, Date Unknown and 1994

The municipal cemetery was laid out in 1878 in response to the overcrowding of local churchyards. Adam Clarke, the mayor's chaplain, remembered in 1883 that only twenty years previously the dead were still buried 'in the closest proximity to the living and with the scantest covering of the earth into which they were restored'. A notable monument in the cemetery is that marking the death of sixty-four miners in the Mossfield Colliery disaster of 1889.

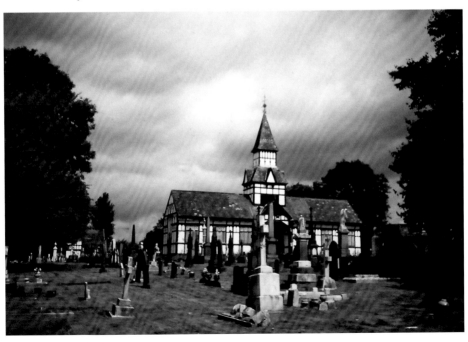

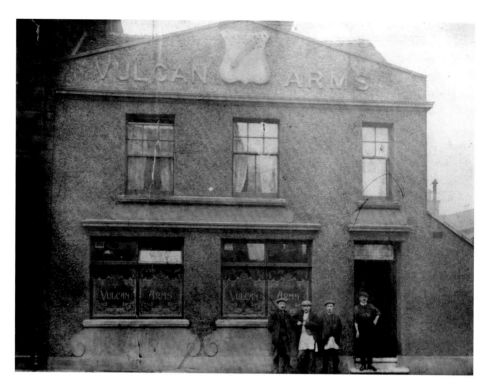

Vulcan Arms, c. 1907, and Same Site, 1979

Potbanks and pubs existed cheek-by-jowl in Longton's industrial heyday; this one's neighbour was the Gladstone Works. Former Gladstone Museum Director Malcolm Hawkesworth remarked to the *Sentinel* newspaper in 1995: 'If you look at any old pottery factory, you will find a pub alongside where the mould runners would be sent to get pots of beer for the kiln firemen.' Like so many pubs in Longton, the Vulcan was a Joule's house.

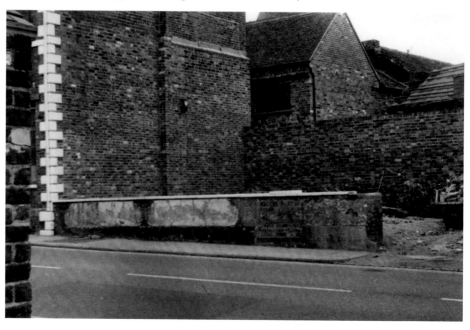

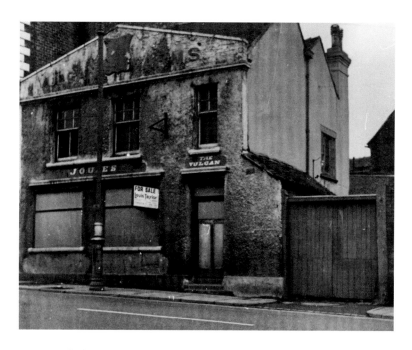

Vulcan Arms, Probably Early 1970s, and Same Site, 1994

Many tipplers found themselves before the Longton police courts, including John Wakefield, who was charged with being drunk and riotous in 1876. What made his case unusual is that he was the proprietor of the Stafford Street Temperance Hotel. He was duly fined 10s and costs. Another temperance establishment was the Longton Coffee House, opened in Market Street in 1880. No alcohol was served, and there were rooms for ladies and non-smokers. Comfortable bedrooms were available for better-off traders seeking accommodation. and chops and steaks were served. Working men could bring their own meals to eat on the premises.

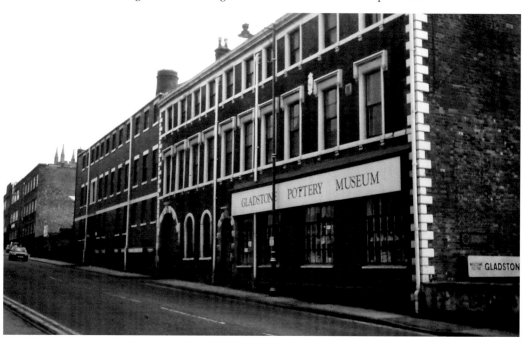

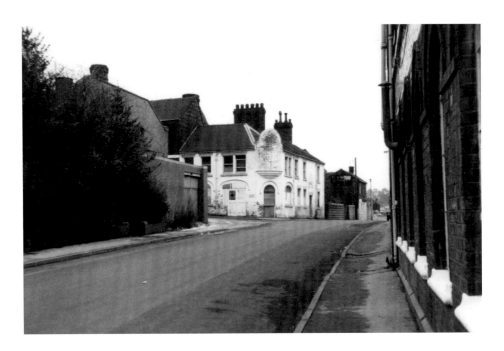

American Inn, *c.* 1980 and 2013

Another pub operating next to a potworks was the American Inn, which stood alongside the Enson Works. The watering hole appears on the 1856 OS map. It closed in 1962. Historians Alan Mansell and Paul Niblett have done much work on the licensing records of the hostelry. In 2012, work began on reconstruction of the building, which is in a conservation area. The intention is to use it as classrooms for the new CORE college next door.

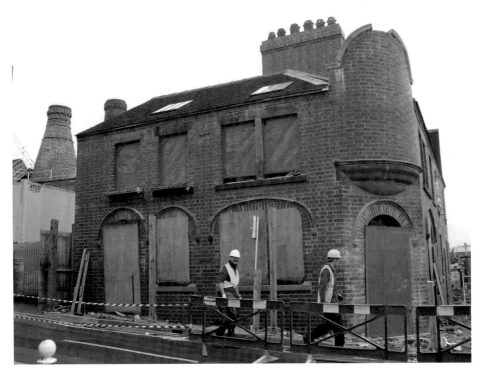

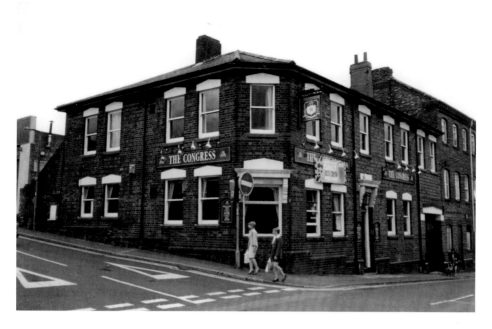

Congress Hotel, 2000 and 2007

The early history of the Congrss Hotel shows that it was involved in local sports. The Congress Football & Athletic Club regularly met there by the 1880s, organising hare and hounds activities. These were essentially cross-country chases. In 2007 the Potteries Pub Preservation group chartered a vintage bus to take its members on a boozy pub crawl of potteries pubs. They were happy to be dropped off at the Congress Hotel in Sutherland Road.

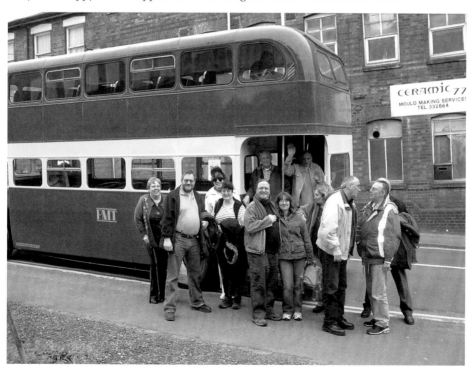

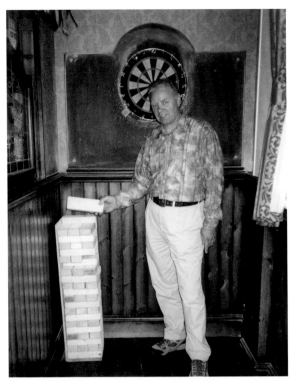

Congress Hotel, 2000 and 2007
Pictured is Dave Scrivens, who had been a policeman based at the station down the road between 1966 and 1982. He recalls that there were smoking concerts at the station's social club twice a year, with entertainment and buffet food on order. However, there was no bar, so the ale was supplied in large jugs by the licensee of the Congress. Dave is seen about to play a game of Jenga. The pub's manageress in 2000 was Clare Nixon. The pub has won many awards over the years, and the present landlord is seen receiving a certificate from Harold Harper, the chairman of the Potteries Pub Preservation group.

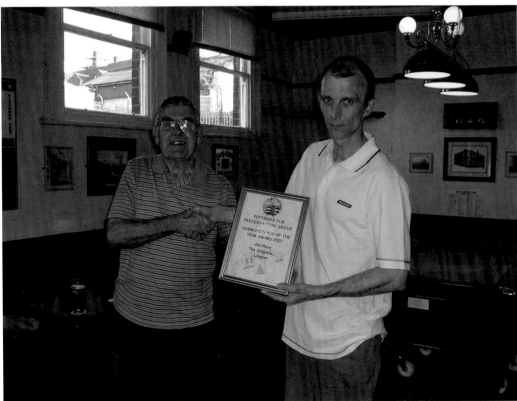

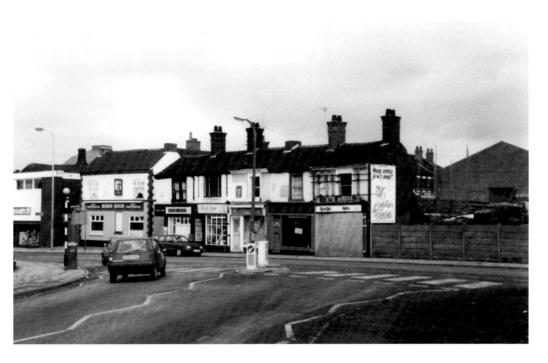

Robin Hood, *c.* 1980 and 1994
This now demolished hostelry stood in The Strand, near to Lightwood Road. The author's pub log for December 1990 recorded that this rather shabby pub boasted a small, dimly-lit lounge with a creased carpet and a redundant disc jockey's podium. The equally small bar incorporated a pool table and a television.

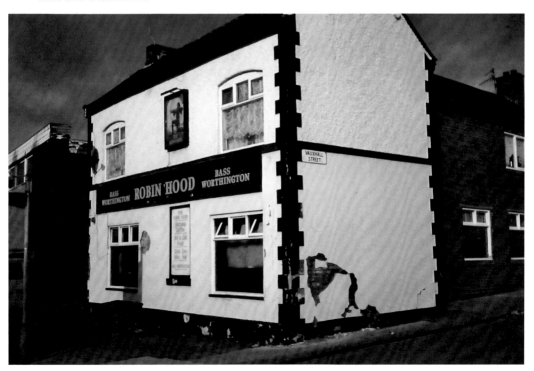

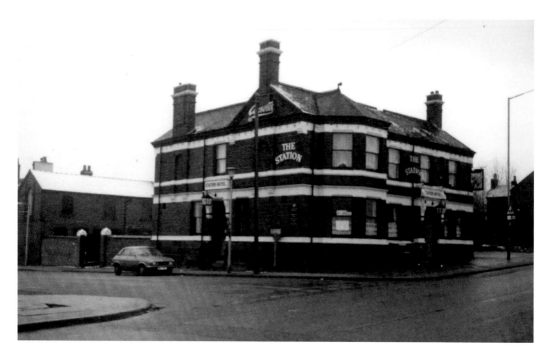

Station Hotel, 1991, and Same Site, 1994

The station hotel in Normacot was still trading in 1991 but was demolished in June 1994, being in the way of the proposed A50 bypass. More than 200 houses were also knocked down. The last licensee was Brian Holt. The pub formerley stood on the corner of Uttoxeter Road and Station Road, to the side of the building. Its name recalls Normacot railway station.

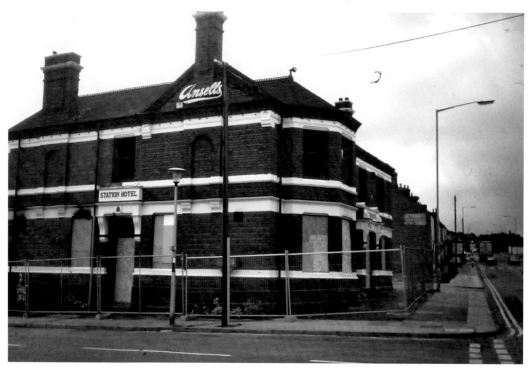

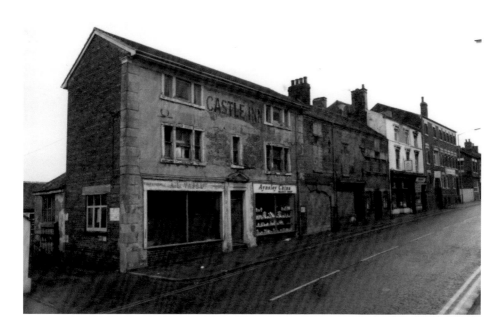

Former Castle Inn, *c.* 1980, and Same Site, 2013

The Castle Inn at Lane End (proprietor James Kettle) is one of the Longton pubs listed in Parsons & Bradshaw's trade directory of 1818. White's trade directory of 1834 listed twenty public houses and sixty beerhouses in Longton and Lane End – fewer than in neighbouring areas of Hanley (forty-three and ninety-one) and Burslem (thirty-six and eighty-two), but more than in Tunstall/Goldenhill (eight and thirty-one), Fenton (ten and twenty-two) and Stoke (fifteen and thirty-six). The Castle's publican by 1863 was J. Adams.

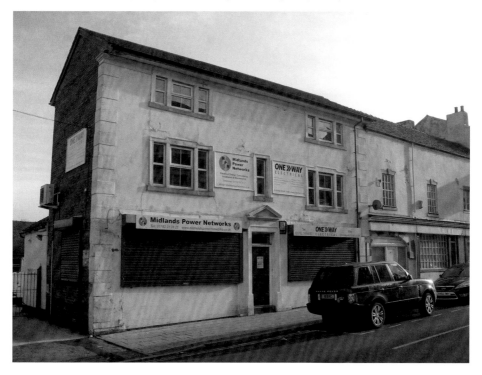

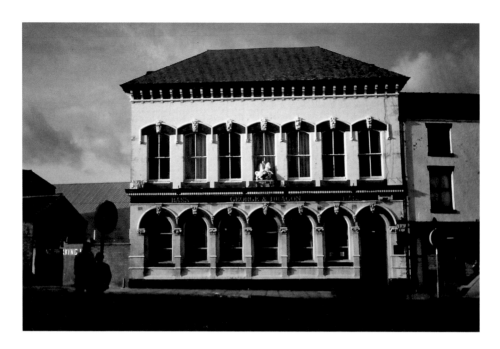

George & Dragon, 1994 and 2012

At the time the above photograph was taken, a Constable print hung at the far end of the rather spartan front bar, overlooking the Strand. This room used to be full of cigarette-smoking, down-at-heel regulars, who would often bring their dogs in. Known with typical Longton iconoclasm as the Owd 'Ut – in spite of its obvious architectural merits – the pub reopened in 2008 after years of standing derelict.

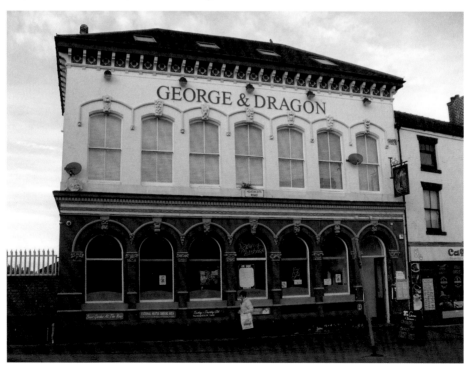

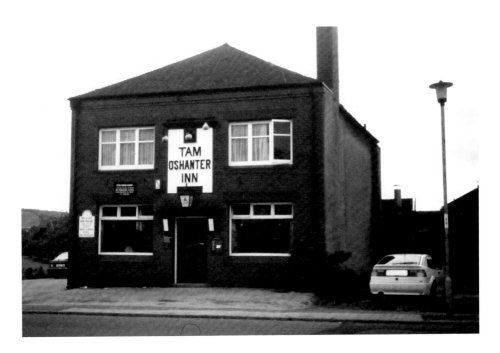

Tam O'Shanter, 1994 and 2012

The proximity of pubs to industry sometimes led to disastrous consequences. In March 1860, Alvah Copestake had been drinking in several pubs in the town, and his delicate condition persuaded two friends to walk him part of the way home. Unfortunately, the next morning his dead body was found in the unprotected marl pit about 30 yards from his home. He was found with his left hand in his trouser pocket and his tobacco box between his fingers.

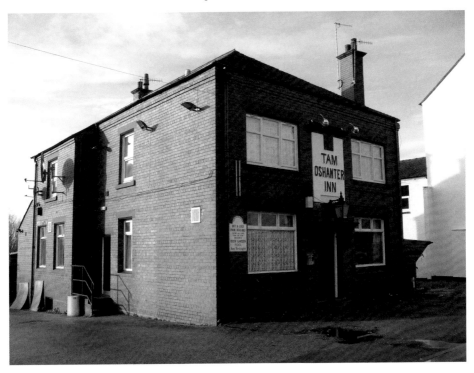

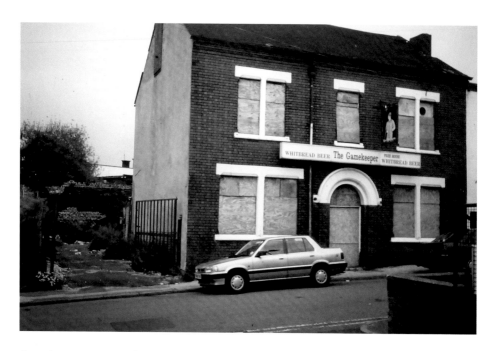

Gamekeeper, 1997 and 2012

In the late 1980s, this pub changed its name from the Trialsmen to the Gamekeeper. A visit in December 1990 revealed a dartboard in the bar section of the pub and lounge bric-a-brac that included pictures of hunting scenes and a large portrait of the Queen. The premises became vacant in 1995 and has since survived fire damage and neglect to remain standing in 2013.

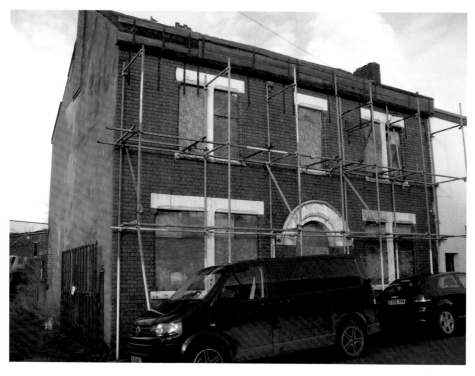

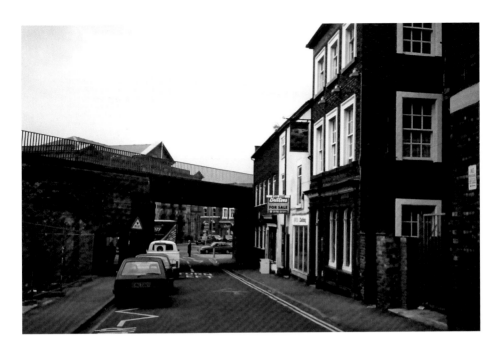

Roebuck, 1997, and Present Site, 2013

This Caroline Street pub used to boast Joule's etched windows. John Joule & Sons Ltd was based in High Street, Stone. The company owned many pubs in the Potteries, where its highest concentration of hostelries was in nearby Longton. Other ex-Joule's houses in the town included the now-demolished Robin Hood, the Union Hotel – now an office building that still bears the old Joule's cross insignia – and the surviving Congress in Sutherland Road.

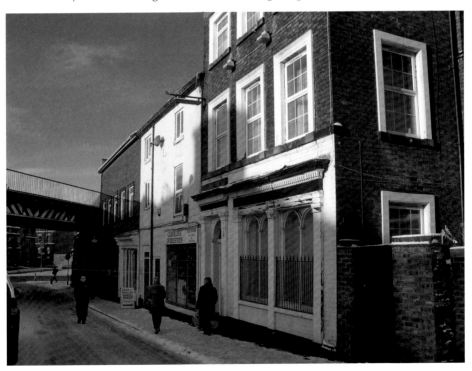

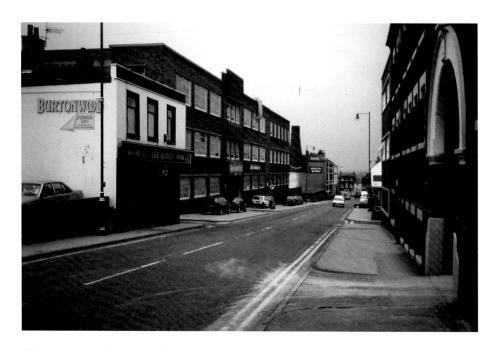

Albion, 1997, and Present Site, 2013
The CAMRA Potteries pub guide for 1984 described the Albion in Uttoxeter Road as a modernised, open-plan pub with a pool table in one room and darts in another. The claim was made that it was one of the twelve most haunted pubs in England! The pub, near to the Gladstone Pottery Museum, had been closed and boarded up for some time prior to being bulldozed in May 2003.

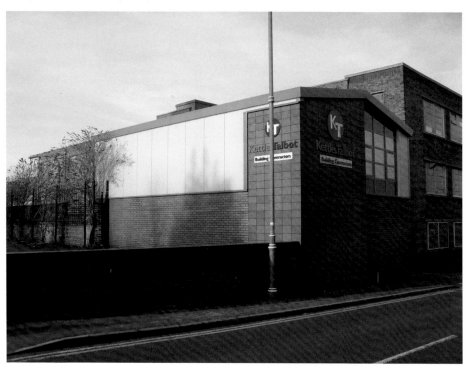

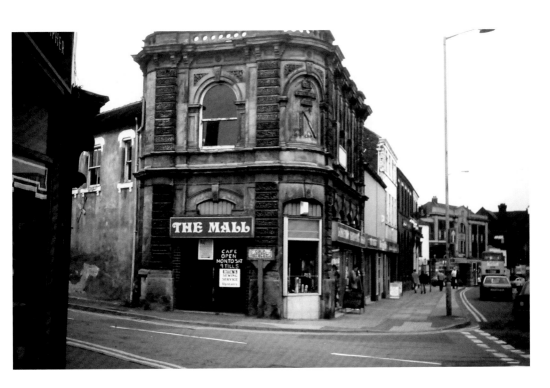

Former Cricketers Arms, 1997 and 2013

The Cricketers Arms stopped trading as a pub long ago, but it was one of several town-centre pubs that helped to fuel debates about the effects of the 'demon drink'. A notorious drunkard and troublemaker, Elizabeth Chadwick had already been convicted eighty-six times before she was charged with being drunk and refusing to leave Longton police office in 1870. The police had no option but to accommodate her in one of the police cells.

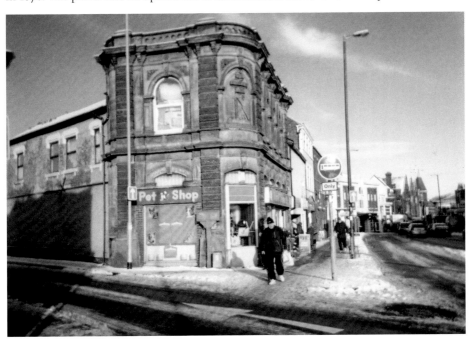

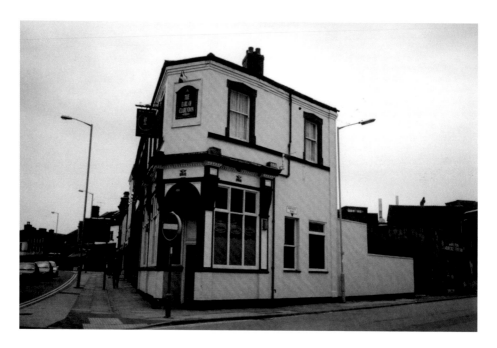

Earl of Clarendon, 1997 and 2013

This former hostelry's name recalled Edward Hyde (1609–74), the first Earl of Clarendon, who was an English politician and historian. He changed sides during the run-up to the Civil War. After initially opposing Charles I's unconstitutional actions, he then became loyal to the Crown. The pub briefly 'enjoyed' a spell as Hickory's, during which time it was nicknamed the Clock by Longton people.

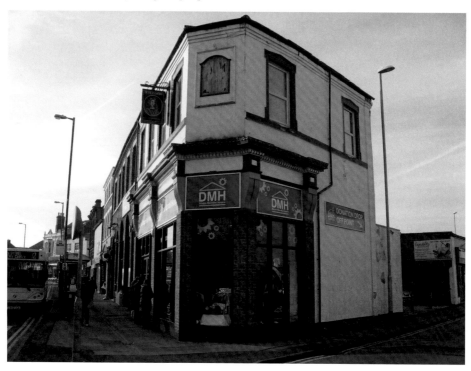

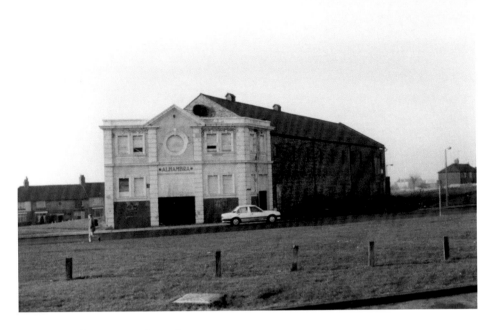

Alhambra Cinema, *c.* 1989 and 1994

Still on the theme of leisure, here is the Alhambra cinema, standing next to terraced houses in Normacot. It was purpose-built in 1914 and owned by pottery manufacturer T. C. Wild. Early patrons sat on wooden benches. The cinema closed in 1977 with a screening of *Magnum Force*, and its removal paved the way for road reconstruction. Doughty building preservationist Angie Stevenson persuaded the powers that be to dismantle the façade in 1994 with a view to future erection elsewhere.

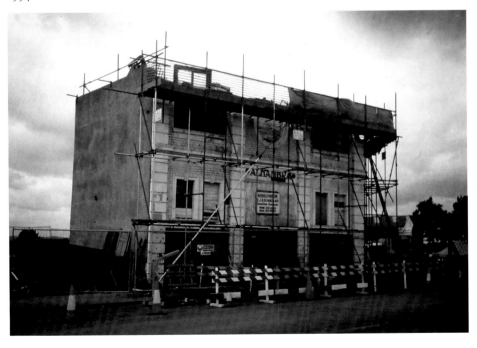

Acknowledgments

The Gladstone Pottery Museum (especially), ATV television, Barewall Art Gallery, Elsie Brown, J. Drury, Ken Edwards, Mrs Gallagher, Roger Harris, R. Lawton, the Lovatt Collection and Staffordshire Past Tracks, Keith Meeson, Ewart Morris, Philip-John Rowley, the *Sentinel* newspaper, Tony Simcock, Stoke-on-Trent City Council, Joe Toriati, Gary Tudor, Keith Warburton, Jim Worgan, Elieen Hallam, and Williamson's photographers in the Strand.

Every effort has been made to correctly identify copyright owners of the photographic material in this book. If, inadvertently, credits have not been correctly acknowledged, we apologise and promise to do so in the author's forthcoming title for Amberley.

Much caption information was personally supplied by the above people. Readers are asked to allow for minor errors of memory.

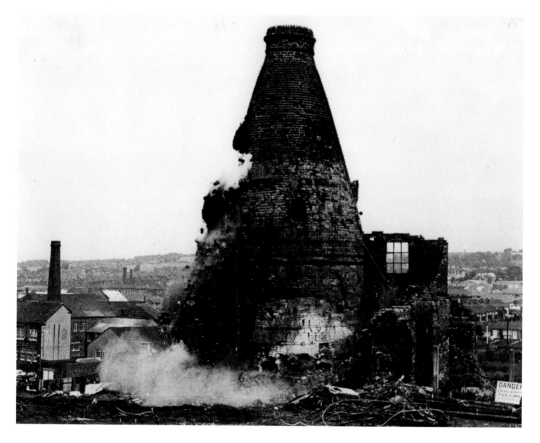

Blue Bell Pottery Demolition, 1975
The demolition of the Blue Bell Pottery was featured in an ITV Midlands documentary. Its producer was Donald Shingler. The show was later screened on the national television network. Mr Shingler and his team also filmed at the Gladstone Pottery Museum.